Mission:

A Cold War Remembrance

by

Thomas Wyckoff LTC, US Army (Ret.)

DORRANCE
PUBLISHING CO
EST. 1920
PITTSBURGH, PENNSYLVAN A 15238

Dorrance Publishing Co
585 Alpha Drive
Pittsburgh, PA 15238
Visit our website at *www.dorrancebookstore.com*

ISBN: 978-1-4809-8685-5
eISBN: 978-1-4809-9205-4

Dedication

"Never forget!
There are 100,000 of them
And fourteen of us—and they have guns!"
MAJ Paul Nelson
USMLM Liaison Officer

And how can a man die better
Than facing fearful odds
For the ashes of his fathers
And the temples of his gods.
Lord MaCauley
from the *Lays of Ancient Rome*

This book is dedicated
to my friend,
Nick Nicholson
Who died unarmed
Facing those fearful odds.

And to my friend Paul Nelson
who died before his time.

Abbreviations and Acronyms

USMLM	US Military Liaison Mission
BRIXMIS	British Military Liaison
FMLM	French Military Liaison Mission
SMLM	Soviet Military Liaison Mission
SERB	Soviet External Relations Branch
USAREUR	US Army, Europe
GSFG	Group of Soviet Forces, Germany
MRD	Motorized Rifle Division
GMRD	Guards Motorized Rifle Division
TD	Tank Division
GTD	Guards Tank Division
SA	Shock Army
GTA	Guards Tank Army
GAD	Guards Artillery Division
USEUCOM	US European Command
PRA	Permanent Restricted Area
TRA	Temporary Restricted Area
MRS	Mission Restricted Area Sign
Sov	Soviet
NARC	Derogative Term for East German Security forces
Stassi	East German Security similar to Soviet KGB
SPETZNAZ	Spetzialnaya Nazncheniya (Soviet equivalents to US Army Rangers)
ROTC	Reserve Officer Training Corp
NPS	Naval Postgraduate School
USARI	US Army Russian Institute
DLI	Defense Language Institute
BMP	Soviet tracked armored personnel carrier
BTR	Soviet multi-axled wheeled armored personnel carrier
BRDM	Soviet two-axled armored scout vehicle

GSFG Ground Order of Battle Circa 1984 – Major Units

1GTA (Dresden)
  9GTD (Riesa)
  11GTD (Dresden)
  20MRD (Grimma)

2GTA (Furstenburg)
  16GTD (Neustrelitz)
  21GMRD (Perleberg)
  94GMRD (Schwerin)
  207MRD (Stendal)

3SA (Magdeburg)
  7GMRD (Dessau)
  10GTD (Altengrabow)
  12GTD (Neuruppin)
  47GTD (Hillersleben)

8GA (Weimar/Nohra)
  27GMRD (Halle)
  39GMRD (Ohrdruf)
  57GMRD (Naumburg)
  79GTD (Jena)

20GA (Eberswalde)
  25GTD (Vogelsang)
  32GTD (Jueterbog)
  35MRD (Krampnitz)
  90GTD (Bernau)

34GAD (Potsdam)

Independent Assault Brigade (Airborne) (Cottbus)

GSFG HQ (Zossen—Wuensdorf)

Prologue

Luck. That's how I got there. Some men plan their lives, always with a goal in mind, always plotting, planning for that next step that takes them to a new level in the effort to attain their life's goals. Not me, I'm just lucky. Or maybe it was something else. I'm a Christian and I believe that God intervenes in men and women's lives. So maybe this was one of those times in my life. Whatever the reason, I certainly didn't set out in life with an objective of working at the US Military Liaison Mission to the Soviet Forces (USMLM) in East Germany. Some military guys did.

The work performed by the officers and men of USMLM and the British and French equivalents was legendary within the US and British Intelligence communities. US intelligence officers fought to get there. For intelligence officers, assignments to the Mission carried great weight in promotion evaluations and career progression. An officer who had served at the Mission commanded immediate respect when present in a gathering of intelligence specialists.

But I was an infantry officer. At the time of my assignment to USMLM, I had only a vague and general idea of what the Mission was all about and what USMLM personnel really did—most of that based on a single TDY trip to visit Berlin a year before my assignment. Yet, in the long run, it proved to be the most personally challenging and rewarding job I have ever had.

The Mission is gone now, only a footnote in the history of that long conflict between the West and the Soviet Union that continued for over forty years following World War II. As that conflict fades into history, I find that my memories of my assignment are also beginning to fade. My memories are personal. I was a Soviet specialist for nearly my whole military career. As a *worker bee*, I was involved in a number of politically important interactions between the Soviet Union and the United States over those years. But for me, the memories of the Mission are not about political events, they are the memories of the people that I worked with, the challenges we faced, the excitement, the camaraderie, and the fears. I'll let the historians tell the world what it all meant. My goal is to try to capture what it felt like to be there. Call it a poor man's view of history.

So this is not an historical document nor does it aspire to be. It is simply the personal recollections of four years of my life at a special place in a special time. I hope that others who also served at the Mission will find bits and pieces of their own experiences intertwined within my recollections. I hope it helps keep their memories alive. For those who weren't there, I hope the book is a somewhat entertaining read and helps them to understand why those of us who did serve at the US Military Liaison Mission to the Soviet Forces in Germany remain so loyal to the memory.

I have done the best that I could to portray the events described in this book as accurately as I could. Others checked some of the details of my stories and offered corrections where appropriate. Where there was a conflict between their memory and mine, my memory ruled. After all, it's my book. Therefore, all errors of fact are the fault of the author. In some cases, I have offered opinions as to why or how we did something. My opinion may be incorrect, but, as it is only an opinion, I do not apologize. It reflects what I thought and felt at the time.

Chapter 1

Perspective

"It's a bust, Jesse. They're gone."

Major Nick Nicholson kicked at the still smoldering campfire in disgust. Nearing the end of his assignment at the U.S. Military Liaison Mission (USMLM) to the Group of Soviet Forces, Germany (GSFG), Nick was hoping that one of his last tours would generate a major intelligence hit. He probably only had three or four tours remaining before he would move on to a next assignment. "Tours" sounded touristy, an understatement for what was one of the most intense intelligence collection efforts staged daily by USMLM and the British and French Allied Military Liaison Missions against the Soviet forces stationed in East Germany. But it was clear that, today, there would be no big hit on the Soviet Forces that had been conducting division level combat training for over a week at the North Elbe River crossing sites just outside of the small town of Havel. They were gone.

Staff Sergeant Jesse Schatz nodded from his post standing up through the open hatch of the highly modified Mercedes Gelandewagon. One of USMLM's most experienced tour NCOs, it was clear to him as well. The action was over. The Sovs were gone. He was disappointed too. tours were a lot more interesting when the Sovs were out in force. When they were quiet, it just meant a lot of patrolling and very little sleep for up to forty-eight hours. Sovs meant excitement, and excitement meant that the time passed quickly.

"What do you want to do now, sir?"

Jesse knew that they had plenty of other targets to cover, but this had been the primary target. If the Sovs had still been there they might have spent the entire tour working the exercise area.

"Well let's poke around a little bit more and then we'll work our way north." Nick shook his head again.

Jesse watched as Nick worked his way through the now abandoned bivouac site, kicking at dying fires, and looking for any refuse left behind to give some indication of the units that might have been involved. As Nick wandered about at various distances from the G-Wagon, Jesse kept watch on the most likely avenues of approach and plotted escape routes in case they should need them. Experienced as he was with more than four hundred tours under his belt, he knew that at the most apparently benign moments things could go bad. He kept an eye on Nick, ready to move to him on a second's notice if necessary to get him back inside the relative safety of the G-Wagon. It wasn't hard to keep an eye on Nick. The major had left his Battle Dress Uniform (BDU) hat inside the vehicle and, at six foot one inches tall, Jesse could clearly see his bright blond curly hair moving through the carefully manicured East German forest.

The tour began with high hopes. Earlier the staff of GSFG had declared a series of Temporary Restricted Area (TRA) notices that, combined with several Permanent Restricted Areas (PRA), stretched from the Lieberosa Training Area near the Polish border through the Altengrabow, Jueterbog, and Letzlinger-Heide Training Areas, ending at the North Elbe River Crossing sites. When they did this, it almost always indicated a major training exercise with substantial elements of at least one division, sometimes two or three, participating. Mission personnel were bound to observe to the letter the terms and limitations of TRAs—generally meaning that, for the duration of the TRA, tours could not enter the temporary restricted areas. tours were permanently restricted from the PRAs. Issuing TRAs was a part of the GSFG general staff checklist when preparing for an exercise. But it seemed that often it was a low priority among the many planning details for major exercises, and, occasionally, the notice was lost in the shuffle and never delivered, or, more frequently, the dates of the exercise changed but the staff forgot to modify the initial TRA notification.

USMLM planned on this forgetfulness. Teams patrolled the area designated to fall within a TRA up to the very last moment before the TRA took effect, hoping to monitor units arriving early into the exercise area. Throughout the duration of the TRAs, USMLM tours prowled the edges of the TRAs and PRAs looking for exercise activity that accidentally or intentionally fell outside of the restricted areas. They loitered at the very edge of the TRAs as they expired and rushed into the areas to try to catch parts of the exercise or units that had not yet left the area.

This had been Nick's hope. The current exercise had been under way for over a week. The TRA blocking access to known bivouac sites northeast of Havel was scheduled to expire on March 24, 1985 at 0600 local time. He and Jesse had launched from USMLM headquarters in West Berlin at 0100, crossed into East Germany via the Glienicke Bridge, stopped by the "official" headquarters of USMLM in Potsdam to pick up food supplies for the trip, and had been on East German Route 5 north to Havel by 0230—plenty of time to work their way to Kummernitz at the northeast edge of the TRA by 0530. There, they checked along the edges of the TRA for any activity and then pulled off into the woods for coffee for a half-hour while waiting for the TRA to formally end.

As they had traveled through Potsdam, they passed various garrisons of the 34th Guards Artillery Division and 35th Motorized Rifle Division. All quiet, but the Missions already knew that these units had not been involved in the exercise, as they were monitored by all of the Missions on a daily basis. No, Nick's hope was that the divisions involved in the exercise were from the 1st Guards Army—already known to be heavily outfitted with the newest military hardware being deployed to Soviet forces in East Germany.

As Nick returned to the G-Wagon, Jesse dropped back down inside from his post standing in the driver's seat through the vehicle overhead hatch, secured the roof latch, and reached across the vehicle to unlock the door for Nick.

"Well, they've been here. There are tracks all over the place. But they cleaned it up pretty well. I couldn't find anything." Nick was disappointed but already moving his thinking to his next target.

"Where to next?" Jesse asked.

Before departing on the mission, he had run through all the assigned targets, reviewing the target folders for each site to get the latest Allied Mission reports from each location, but, planning-wise, he and Nick had focused on the river-crossing site. Except for noting the latest developments at each site in the target folders, it didn't make much difference to Jesse what the sequence was anyhow. He knew East Germany and the access and egress routes around each scheduled target like the back of his own hand.

"I want to get to Neubukow up by Rostock by dark, but let's hit Ludwigslust next."

USMLM teams were authorized to follow any activity that they happened upon, but covering garrisons and bivouac sites was strictly regulated to avoid unanticipated overlap by two teams at the same target. Nick's targets were generally on a line from Havel on north through several sites in Ludwigslust, on to garrisons of the 94th Guards Motorized Rifle Division near Schwerin, the Neubukow Air Defense Training site on the north coast, the military port facilities in Rostock, and ending with a sweep through the eastern part of East Germany on the team's return south. By plan, the team would cover around 1500 kilometers before the tour was over and return to USMLM headquarters in West Berlin late on 25 March.

Jesse headed the G-Wagon north away from Havel along Route 107 back to Route 5 where they turned northwest toward Ludwigslust. The unit stationed at Ludwigslust was a Motorized Rifle Regiment of the 21st Motorized Rifle Division. The garrison itself was within a Permanent Restricted Area, although located on a boundary road that allowed USMLM tours to do periodic "drive-byes" to see if anything was going on at the garrison. Nearby were two local training areas, both outside the PRA. One was directly across the road from the garrison to the southeast. The larger of the two was across Route 5 to the northeast. The team's task was a low-key check at all three locations for any activity. Jesse drove northwest along Route 5 passing north of Grabow before turning west on a small dirt road that he knew would take them to the smaller of the two training areas.

"Let's go slow and quiet, Jesse."

Both Nick and Jesse stepped up their visual search for any military vehicles or personnel that might monitor their approach to the training area. Of interest in the training area was a vehicle storage shed at the west end capable of holding up to eight tank or self-propelled artillery sized vehicles. From previous observations, USMLM analysts knew that this garrison often received new equipment early and was used to train other units in the area. The training area and the shed often held such equipment, and, this being a Sunday morning, both were likely to be unattended. Training equipment was sometimes parked in the open and simply covered with tarps. During his preparations, Nick had noted that during the previous summer a team from the French Military Liaison Mission (FMLM) had been fired at by training area guards as they attempted to examine a tarped vehicle parked in the middle of the training area. A number of teams had been to the site since, with no incidents occurring.

"Do you want to work our way over to Route 191 and do a drive-by of the garrison and then turn into the training area? Or do you want to do the training area first?" Jesse asked as they approached a turn leading through a small, forested area.

"Let's go direct to the training area. If we run the garrison wall first, someone will see us for sure and we won't have much time at either of the training areas. Get me someplace where we can see the vehicle shed and the guard post from the wood line." Nick followed their progress on his 1:50,000 scale map to make sure that he knew exactly where they were and how quickly they were coming up on the training area.

As they moved forward, Jesse slowed the vehicle until they were moving forward at a creep. He didn't need the map. He had been to the training area many times and knew they were very close to the southern edge. Rather than follow the trail directly to the edge of the training area, he turned into the woods and worked his way forward to where they were positioned behind some bushes with a view of much of the training area. The equipment shed was about 150 meters to their left. The training area was not large and extended to their right another five hundred or six hundred meters. It was about two hundred meters wide.

Nick pulled out his binoculars and surveyed the training area. To the right of the vehicle shed, he could see the guard shack alongside the trail that led through the woods northwest to the garrison. Though only about three hundred meters beyond, the garrison was not visible through the woods. He spent several minutes surveying the training area. Not much of interest—the shed was closed up tight, no training in progress, nothing going on that could be seen. Nick was tempted by the shed but thought better of it for the moment.

"Not much going on here either, Jesse. Let's go check the other training area. Maybe there is something going on there."

In their hearts, neither believed there would be but being thorough was part of the job.

Jesse carefully backed the vehicle back into the wood line and worked his way back to the trail. They reversed their route back along the dirt trail to Route 5 and then turned north. The entrance to the second and larger training area was not far away, just north of the intersection between Route 5 and Route 191.

• • •

Junior Sergeant Alexander Ryabtsev sat leaning against a tree almost directly across the training area from where he had observed the Mission vehicle pull up to the edge of the wood line. As he saw the vehicle, he flopped over into a prone position to watch. He recognized the vehicle. He had seen them before, and the commander of the guard had warned him to be alert for vehicles from the foreign *missiya*. They were known to visit the unit training areas every so often.

He was supposed to be at the guard post near the sheds but he knew that no one would come to check on him until time to change the guards and that would not be for a considerable while.

He watched the Mission vehicle, not sure what he should do. He knew the vehicle and the people inside should not be there. But his instructions on what to do about it were not very precise. He decided to wait and see what happened. What he was sure about was that if someone discovered that these "spies" had been here and he had done nothing, he would be at fault, particularly if someone noted that he had not been at his proper guard post. Last summer, a warrant officer and another sergeant had seen personnel from one of these vehicles tampering with one of his unit's vehicles that had been parked in the training area. The warrant had unleashed a volley of shots from his handgun at the intruders. The missiya crew had escaped but a great deal was made in the garrison of the successful deterrent.

He stood in the wood line behind a tree and took aim at the vehicle. He hesitated, wondering if he should shoot. As he watched, the vehicle backed into the woods and disappeared.

He sat down again, pulled out a cigarette and wondered if he really could have pulled the trigger. He noted with some pride that his hands were steady as he lit his cigarette.

He thought to himself, "Yes, Junior Sergeant Ryabtsev, I think you could pull the trigger. If you had to."

• • •

Nick looked at his watch. It was 1330, and still nothing was going on. It was not surprising, even the Sovs took Sundays off unless there was an exercise going on. But the exercise had been a bust and likely did not involve any of the divisions from the 2nd Guards Tank Army from the northwestern region of East Germany where Nick's tour was now targeted. Nick was also pretty sure that the Schwerin area was going to be quiet also.

"Maybe we can get something productive from this tour yet," Nick thought.

Not only was he a tour officer but he was also the senior intelligence officer in USMLM Ground Section. Although covering a river-crossing exercise was a lot more exciting, gathering technical intelligence was also important. Close-up handheld photography of new equipment or variants was always of value—worth going after and worth reporting. Sometimes, first time coverage of a new important piece of equipment was as or more valuable than catching the entire order of battle of a unit as it moved into or out of an exercise area. He briefly thought about the week that he and Staff Sergeant Jim McDowell had spent hiding in the Koenigsbruek Training Area north of Dresden unsuccessfully trying to capture the first handheld photography of the new Soviet T-80 tank.

"Let's go back to the other training area and take another look at the sheds." Jesse nodded *okay* and began retracing their steps. This time, as he approached the first training area, he did not turn off into the wood line but pulled directly to the edge of the training area from the trail. They again halted and surveyed the area and, again, saw no one.

"Let's get closer to the shed."

"Let me circle it once to make sure that the guard isn't on the back side. I'll park where I can see anyone approaching up the trail from the garrison and also two sides of the shed."

Jesse pulled forward at a relatively slow speed, both he and Nick searching the wood line; but mostly focused on the shed, the area around the guard post, and the trail leading northwest to the garrison. Jesse drove completely around the sheds and close to the guard shack so that they could peer inside. No one around.

"Okay, I'm going to get out here. Make sure you keep me in sight." Nick grabbed his pocket camera and opened the door.

The G-Wagon was about forty meters from the shed. As Nick got out, Jesse maneuvered the G-Wagon into a position that gave him maximum visual coverage of the most likely approach routes. The worst case was that a vehicle would drive quickly up the access trail from the garrison giving him little time to get the G-Wagon secured and started, and to link up with the major before the approaching vehicle was on them. He positioned the vehicle to give himself maximum reaction time. Jesse glanced to his left rear and could see that Major Nicholson was fairly close the shed. He turned off the engine, opened the top hatch, and stood up.

. . .

Junior Sergeant Ryabtsev had drifted off to sleep. Despite the fact that it was still March it was a warm, sunny day, and he had no reason not to allow himself to take a short nap. He didn't awaken until he heard a vehicle door shut. It wasn't loud but distinct. It sounded like the commander of the guard getting out of his UAZ-469 (Soviet equivalent of a military jeep). Why would he return to the training area so early?

Then, he realized, it was not the commander of the guard. The Mission vehicle was back. Now it was parked near the shed with one of the team members out of the vehicle. Ryabtsev grabbed his rifle and leaped to his feet. He hesitated for a moment—maybe he should shout. No, too late for that.

He threw his AK-47 rifle to his shoulder, flipping the safety off as he had been trained to do. The driver of the vehicle stood up through the vehicle hatch, sixty or seventy meters away—an easy shot. Ryabtsev pulled the trigger. The sound of the shot echoed through the training area. The vehicle driver immediately dropped down through the hatch. Had he hit him? He wasn't sure, but the second intruder had turned and was now running back toward the vehicle. Everything seemed to be happening fast but in slow motion at the same time! He drew a bead on the running figure and pulled the trigger twice. The figure went down.

Now Junior Sergeant Ryabtsev was shaking. He could see that the driver was still sitting up behind the steering wheel of the vehicle although he didn't seem to be moving. The intruder outside the vehicle, now lying face down on the ground, also did not appear to be moving. Ryabtsev began running toward the vehicle, his rifle at the ready.

. . .

Jesse sat, stunned in his seat. As he had stood up in the hatch, he had seen the soldier in the wood line raise his rifle and fire. He heard the whine of the bullet as it whizzed directly over his head. He instinctively dropped into the vehicle, pulled the hatch closed, and secured it. It was not conscious thought, just a reaction. As he latched the roof, he heard the second and third shots. He turned and looked over his shoulder at Major Nicholson just in time to see him go down. Nick was motionless, lying face down in the dirt. Jesse couldn't tell for sure if he was hit or how badly. He froze for a moment. Nothing in his long experience as a driver for USMLM had prepared him for this moment.

Within seconds, he regained control of himself. He could see the soldier running toward the vehicle with his rifle at the ready but slammed the vehicle into reverse and backed up about fifteen meters, so that Nick's form was lying beside the vehicle on the driver's side, still face down.

As Jesse stopped the vehicle and started to get out, Nick raised his head and said, "Jesse, I've been shot." Then his head dropped back, face down, into the dirt. A pool of blood was beginning to spread from under his body.

By this time the soldier had arrived at the vehicle and was gesturing wildly toward Jesse with the AK-47. Jesse reached down and picked up the vehicle first aid kit, clearly marked with a Red Cross, and, holding it up, started to get out of the vehicle. The soldier again gestured wildly with his weapon, this time pointing the AK-47 directly into Jesse's face. Jesse closed the door and looked down at Major Nicholson. Nick did not move.

Within a few minutes, another soldier walked up the access road apparently to determine what the shooting was all about. The second soldier was not in much of a hurry. Soviet soldiers were known to conduct informal target practice with their weapons while on guard duty. Following a very excited discussion, the second soldier jogged back up the trail returning in another few minutes with a Soviet officer.

Again, Jesse held up the first aid kit, and this time the officer gestured for him to remain in the vehicle. He walked to Nick's form and placed his fingers on Nick's neck, looking for a pulse. He looked back at the guard and the G-Wagon and shook his head.

• • •

At around 1500 local time, the office of the GSFG Staff Office, known to the Missions as the Soviet External Relations Branch (SERB), called to notify USMLM that there had been an incident involving a USMLM Liaison team at a Soviet installation near Ludwigslust. SERB requested that the Chief of USMLM, Colonel Roland *Lajoie*, personally come to the scene to investigate the circumstances along with representatives from SERB. It was quickly apparent that the USMLM team involved was Major Nicholson and Staff Sergeant Schatz. They were the only team scheduled to be in that area, and the installations at Ludwigslust were on their secondary target list.

Colonel Lajoie, Lt. Colonel Larry Kelley (USMC), and Staff Sergeant Randy Everett departed from the USMLM headquarters to the site in the Mission Chief's Mercedes 350SL sedan, following much the same route that Nick and Jesse had followed that morning. In the USMLM headquarters, others notified of the request assembled at the Mission to provide any support that might be required. During these early moments, there was no hint of what had occurred. The history of the four Allied Liaison Missions (including the Soviet Military Liaison Mission—SMLM) was replete with complicated situations that had required the presence of senior Mission representatives to verify facts or receive reprimands from Soviet military leaders for perceived infractions of the "rules," such as they were. Such reprimands were not unusual and, based on diplomatic precedent, always rejected or denied by the recipients.

Among those assembled at the USMLM headquarters were Major Paul Nelson, USMLM Executive Officer, Major John Eschrich, Chief of Ground Operations, and Major Tom Wyckoff, Ground Operations Officer. In addition to their assigned responsibilities, all three were long-time, close friends of Nick and each had toured frequently with SSG Schatz. As they waited, they discussed the possibilities. An SMLM team (Soviet equivalent of USMLM but operating in the US Sector of West Germany) had been detained in a US Permanent Restricted Area earlier in the week. Often in such cases, the Soviets would attempt to retaliate by exerting extraordinary effort to "catch" a US team in a compromising situation or, in some extreme cases, by actually staging such an event. The three friends speculated that the current situation might be some form of retaliation. Nick was a careful tour officer. It was not likely that he had been caught in a restricted area, but, because of the proximity of his targets to PRAs, it was not difficult to imagine the Soviets halting the vehicle and dragging it into the restricted area to present in a staged fashion to Colonel Lajoie. Other scenarios could be imagined, but the possibilities were endless. The group just waited.

At 2230, a phone call came from Major Jim Silva, the duty officer at the USMLM Potsdam House. All three friends picked up the phone simultaneously. John Eschrich answered.

Major Silva began, "Colonel Lajoie just called from Ludwigslust. Nick's been shot. He's dead. I'm sorry." Major Silva then noted that SSG Schatz was unharmed and continued with a list of actions and notifications that Colonel LaJoie wanted initiated immediately.

• • •

I hesitated to begin this book with this story. At first, this was simply a gathering of personal recollections—war stories, if you will—about the time that I spent as a liaison officer at the US Military Liaison Mission. At times, the stories have fascinated others when I have chosen to share them. But I am beginning to forget the details and decided that I would try to capture them in a more permanent way.

But as I began to write (and as I have experienced as I related the stories to others), there are two underlying themes to all of my recollections that are difficult to convey.

The first is that we, those of us who served as Mission tour officers and NCOs, were part of a war that continued for forty plus years. A war that was carried out on many fronts and was sometimes hot and sometimes cold. We all knew it was a great war, one with a powerful, worthy opponent. We all lost friends during that war in Korea, in Vietnam, on intelligence missions that even today cannot be mentioned, and other locations. It was a "real war," to quote Richard Nixon, one with real costs and real casualties. There was a victory at the end. There were winners and losers. Our main protagonist no longer even exists. This is the setting in which the Mission operated. The actions of the Mission were on the very cutting edge of the conflict, actually operating behind the lines of the best forces that the Soviet Union had to offer. When I tell stories of my time at the Mission to my nephews and nieces today, it is sometimes difficult for them to understand the context in which the stories occurred. Although never formally declared, the outcome of this conflict was important to the security of our country.

The contributions by the Allied Missions to the successful outcome of that war were immeasurable. When I left the Mission, I had the fortune of being assigned as Chief of the Warsaw Pact Ground Forces Order of Battle Section in the Defense Intelligence Agency. Until that assignment, I did not understand just how important the contribution really was. Good, solid intelligence analysts devoured Mission reporting for insights into the Soviet military forces arrayed against NATO. Mission reports were the most accurate, reliable source of reporting that any DIA or CIA analyst would normally get. Without remembering the setting within which the Missions operated, it is not possible to understand the importance of what tour personnel did and why they were willing to take risks to do it.

The second point is that working at the Mission was dangerous at times. Behind the war stories that always sounded funny or exciting in hindsight, there were often stressful and dangerous situations. For most of us—okay, I will speak only for myself, but I believe that I speak for most—danger was something that you were always conscious of but could never really think about because to think about it was to invite paralyzing fear into situations that could not bear paralysis. You just had to put it aside. And when your assignment to the Mission was all over and you came through it okay, you had to ask yourself, Was there really anything to really be afraid of? Was I just paranoid? Yet many times other liaison officers and I had stood exactly where Nick was killed. Nick's death was a defining moment on a very personal level. It provided the answer definitively and publicly. "Yes. The danger was real."

For me, there were many defining moments during my tour at the Mission. Nick was not the only Mission member killed while I was at the Mission. An East German military truck rammed a French Military Liaison Mission team just a little over a year before Nick's death. The driver, a French NCO, L'adjutant-chef Philippe Marriotti, was killed. The officer with him was in the hospital and recovery for over a year. A number of USMLM teams were rammed, shot at, beaten, and on and on, just in the four years that I was at the Mission I think that, should someone compile a complete listing of the "incidents" involving members of Allied Military Missions over their forty-year life, it might be quite startling. Yet, despite this, at least for the time that I was at the Mission, and with the exception of seven days following Nick's death, there was never a day that the US Military Liaison Mission did not have tour personnel on the road behind the lines in East Germany. The casualties were not only to Mission personnel. In their efforts to deter the activities of Mission personnel, the Soviet and East German military personnel also took risks that sometimes resulted in what will often remain undocumented injuries or worse to themselves. Several such incidents are described in the stories that follow.

Nevertheless, for me, Nick's death was the particular defining moment. From the moment that we began our studies to become Army Soviet Foreign Area Officers (FAO) at the Naval Postgraduate School in Monterey in 1978, we were good friends. When we moved on to the US Army Russian Institute, Nick was my traveling partner on all of our class trips. We lived in apartments across the hall from each other while attending USARI. We got to know each other's families, including parents and siblings. Our families went on ski vacations together. We left the doors to our apartments open during holidays so that we could run back and forth sharing festivities and food. I watched his little girl grow up. As ground operations officer, I sent him on the mission on which he died. For me, his death was not just a news item: it was personal. In this regard, I speak not only for myself but also for four other friends that all served together through schools and several years at the Mission. Nick, Paul Nelson, Clyde Evans, and I all worked together on our master's degrees in National Security Affairs at the Naval Postgraduate School. We all studied Russian together at the Defense Language Institute in Monterey and then for two years at the US Army Russian Institute in Garmisch, Germany. We were joined in Garmisch by John Eschrich. During those times, Nick was the social spark plug of our group. He loved organizing and supporting social events. He helped make our community of students come to life. He was a serious student who knew when to let down and enjoy life. Due to a very unique opportunity, all five of us were selected for assignment to the US Military Liaison Mission at the same time. We grew together. We studied, respected, and fought the Soviet military in our own way in our intelligence-gathering efforts. We loved the Mission. Losing Nick was personal to all of us.

One other aspect of Nick's tragic death became a defining moment. Until his death, outside of the Mission I never talked to anyone about what I did every day when I crossed the border into East Germany. With the press coverage that accompanied Nick's death, the activities of our very secret organization became public. Although warned that our classified status remained and that we were not to discuss our activities, information about the Mission was everywhere on TV, in Newsweek and Time Magazine. From that moment on, parents and family knew what we were doing when we crossed into East Germany and worried in a way that they had not before.

I do not hate the Soviets or Russians for what happened. I don't think Nick would have either. It was a war. Unexpected, tragic things happen during wars. This was one of those events. liaison teams intentionally operated in a gray area of legitimate activities. Operating in gray areas always carries risks. At the Mission our greatest successes were always within that poorly defined gray area of activity. There were rules and unwritten rules that were not clearly defined by either side except in a very sparsely-worded agreement called the "Huebner-Malinin Agreement." At USMLM, we knew that we stretched the limits of that agreement and we knew that the Soviets did their best to contain our efforts. Their efforts to contain our activities were carried out by young soldiers and officers with little guidance, but armed with loaded rifles. Risk was inherent in the activities in which we engaged, and liaison personnel consciously accepted the risks. To me, it was somewhat of a miracle that the Missions had operated for all of those years without a similar incident occurring earlier.

Nick was a student of the Soviet Union. He studied to understand what motivated them to find common ground. He was fascinated by Russian culture. When we traveled together in the Soviet Union and Eastern Europe, he was always seeking opportunities to talk to Soviet citizens to better understand them and their government. What made us friends was that we both believed that, over time, the Soviet Union would change. We speculated that it would take a hundred years. It has changed much faster. I like to believe that the confrontation that occurred between the political leaders of the United States and the Soviet Union following Nick's death was one of those events that spurred the rapid changes leading to the disintegration of the Soviet Union. Others have written to the political implications and ramifications that resulted from Nick's death. I am glad that they have, and I believe that they have done a good job. I want to believe that Nick's death was not in vain and that his loss to his family and to his friends made a difference.

Other than the notes above, this book is neither a political commentary nor a history of the Mission. The stories that follow are written as personal memories. For those who are interested, they also may help the reader to understand why an American Army major was killed on a sunny afternoon in March 1985, outside of a small Soviet military garrison in Ludwigslust, East Germany. I hope the stories are fascinating and entertaining to all who read it. But to really understand them, you have to remember that they were all within the context of a real war between the United States and the Soviet Union. And the danger was real.

Chapter 2
Selection

Most of my assignments while serving in the Army were not my first choice. As a Christian, I believe that God has played a role in guiding my life, and I have to say that, regardless of the fact that I was not often successful in selecting my assignments, I never had an assignment in the Army that was not professionally satisfying and personally rewarding. I thank God for this. When I first joined the Army in 1972, I wanted to be an armor officer, and I wanted to serve in West Germany where I had lived as a kid while my father served there in the Air Force. I wound up in the infantry. I was a Reconnaissance Platoon Leader in the Combat Support Company, 1st Battalion, 60th Infantry (Go Devils), 172nd Infantry Brigade (Arctic, Light, Airmobile); Company Commander of the Personnel Company in the 172nd's Support Battalion; Rifle Company Executive Officer, Infantry Battalion Adjutant, and Rifle Company Commander all back in the 1st of the 60th—all at Fort Richardson, Alaska; and all great jobs. I got to shoot every type of weapon the infantry had, threw hand grenades until my arm was sore, was sent to special schools to learn to ski and climb mountains, and enjoyed the privilege of working with soldiers every day. I loved the infantry. I loved Alaska. I made friends that I still treasure today. I thank God that I didn't get my first choice.

On completion of my time with the 172nd, I knew I was likely to be assigned to one of the Army's three Rs—duty with a Reserve unit, Recruiting Command, or ROTC duty. Having become enthralled with skiing while I was in Alaska, I did some research and made up a list of fifteen universities with Army ROTC programs within a one-hour drive of a major ski area. When the assignments guys talked to me about my next assignment, I was going to be ready. When they asked what I wanted to do, I was going to say, "Well, I'd like to work on my master's degree." I was sure the response was going to be, "Boy, do we have a good deal for you—how about an ROTC assignment where you can get your master's degree?" At which point I was prepared to whip out my list of fifteen universities and strike a deal for a school near a great ski area.

It didn't unfold that way. When I said I wanted to get my master's degree, the assignments officer asked if I had heard about the Army Foreign Area Officer (FAO) program. I had but didn't know much about it. He explained how Army officers that had successfully completed their company grade qualification (which I would on completion of the Infantry Officer Advanced Course) were sent to school at a major university to get their master's degree and learn a foreign language. This intrigued me since my undergraduate degree at Oklahoma State University was in political science and I had concentrated heavily on Arab studies. Unfortunately, as my luck would have it (or as God had plans for me), there was no space in the Arabic FAO program. So the assignments officer reeled off a series of other countries that still had vacancies. When he hit Russia I asked for details. He started by describing a two-year program at the Naval Post Graduate School in Monterey, California that included one year at the Defense Language Institute—also in Monterey. Mentally, I calculated that NPS and DLI were about two and a half hours from all of the major Lake Tahoe ski areas. This was an immediate plus. He continued by describing the two-year program at the US Army Russian Institute (USARI) located in Garmisch, Germany. I was an Air Force brat. When my father had been stationed in Germany, our family had vacationed at the US military winter recreation center in Garmisch. So two years within three hours of Lake Tahoe and two years living in Garmisch, Germany, within rock-throwing distance of a ski slope sounded just right. I signed on.

Before I started the formal training program, I had to complete the Infantry Officers Advanced Course at Fort Benning, Georgia. (One point of pride, I graduated number seven in the class—one of ten honor graduates out of 160 infantry captains and majors; like I said, I loved the infantry). Only once did I question my decision to commit to the Soviet FAO program. As I attended IOAC, I began calculating the number of years that I would spend away from the infantry. Two years at graduate school and DLI, then two years at USARI, followed by a mandatory two-year utilization tour where the Army made use of all of the training that I would have received—a total of six years away from my basic branch. This would probably kill my infantry career. However, during one session at IOAC, a general officer addressed the class. He discussed probable career progression and noted that only one out of ten officers currently present in the room would likely ever command an infantry battalion—lousy odds from my perspective. I knew what all of the other jobs were like as an infantry officer, and, to me, they were just the price you had to pay to get to be a battalion commander. Even then, as a battalion commander, I would command in an era in which I really hoped there would never be a war. With those prospects, I decided I might make a better contribution in the Army as a FAO.

I spent the next six months at the Army's Foreign Area Officers Training Course at Ft. Bragg, North Carolina. Most of the officers in attendance were learning skills that would stand them in good stead as they worked as attachés in allied countries. Attachés in most countries worked to coordinate training and military assistance programs or joint military exercises and activities. Soviet FAOs were odd ducks in this environment. They might serve as attachés, but it would be in a much more hostile environment. At the time the FAO course was divided into "seminars" based on geographic regions in which FAOs might be expected to serve (Asia, Africa, Middle East, Latin America). Soviet FAO misfits were spread throughout the various seminars. I was in the African Seminar along with another Soviet FAO, and subsequently career-long friend, Dick Mahlum. The African Seminar actually turned out to be fairly interesting since it was the year that the Soviets and Americans switched sides between Ethiopia and Somalia. It was at the FAO Course that I met a number of Soviet FAOs with whom I would interact over the next fifteen years but also one of the life-long friends that would end up together during my assignment at USMLM—Captain Paul Nelson, accompanied by his wife, Mary. Paul was a big, tall, powerfully-built West Point grad that was in the Adjutant General's Corp due to a serious neck injury incurred in the wrestling program at West Point. I discovered that, despite his neck injury, he was in the FAO program for the right reasons. He was a ski-bum.

At the Naval Post Graduate School, the group of students and friends that would come together and finally graduate in 1982 from USARI really began to form. Paul Nelson, Dick Mahlum, and I were there, but we were now joined by Nick Nicholson, Clyde Evans, Phil Hockensmith, and, in the second year, by about a half dozen others that would go on to USARI. It was a good group—a good mix of serious students and skiers. We had a great three or four years studying and skiing together. The friendships formed here carried on throughout the rest of my professional military career.

I suppose that, I have to confess, I don't consider myself one of the most successful students of Russian language to complete either the Defense Language Institute program or USARI (on the other hand, I am a quite good skier). It was hard for me to adjust to this fact because in other Army schools, other Army assignments, and in athletic events (always a big part of my life) I was very competitive. I worked really hard to do well studying Russian, but ultimately I had to concede that I was just average. In hindsight, it's somewhat funny to me because—subsequently, of all my contemporaries in the Russian language studies program, and although I was only about average in ability—I have probably spent more time consistently using Russian and involved with Russian-speaking people than most of the very good Russian speakers in my class.

The story of my assignment to USMLM actually begins at USARI. USARI was a recruiting ground for USMLM. There was always a pool of fifteen to twenty-five students each year completing their FAO training and Russian language studies. The students were all dealing with assignments officers and facing new assignments at the conclusion of the course. Most would return to Washington to work in the Defense Intelligence Agency, one of the service staffs (Army, Air Force, Navy/Marine Corp), or on the Joint Staff. A few would manage assignments back to their basic branch in route to assignments as attachés in the Soviet Union or one of the Eastern Bloc countries (generally, all Army attachés in these countries were also Russian FAOs). And one or two would be handpicked to work at USMLM.

Students were offered the opportunity to travel to West Berlin and visit the headquarters of USMLM to meet the staff and find out more about what USMLM was all about. All of the student intelligence officers already knew and were lobbying hard for one of these assignments as "plums" in their career field. I took advantage of the TDY trip to West Berlin along with the others because I had never been there and wanted to see this closed city for myself. But, being an average student, I did not hold out much hope for one of the coveted Mission assignments. I had resigned myself to being one of the guys headed for Washington—not a bad assignment from my perspective since my wife and I had visited DC earlier as tourists and enjoyed the visit. I didn't think I had much chance so I didn't interview or press for the assignment when the USMLM recruiting team came to Garmisch in the fall of 1981. Some will call it luck but I will continue to believe that God directs my life. John Boles, a good friend of mine who had graduated from USARI the year before and was, at the time, the Executive Officer at USMLM, called me and asked why I had not interviewed. I ran through the points above and said that I was interested but just thought that the odds were too long and decided to focus on the probable bird in hand (DIA). Again—intervention in my life. It was an unusual moment. USMLM was not looking for two officers this year but five. They wanted a mix of Army specialties, and John thought that as an infantry officer I had a good shot.

Honestly, I still didn't have a good picture in my mind of what I was getting into, but both Dru and I had enjoyed the two years in Germany, and a follow-on assignment, particularly in Berlin, sounded good. Despite my week of TDY at the USMLM in the previous fall, I had only a vague idea of what liaison officers did. But DIA didn't sound nearly as interesting as an assignment in West Berlin, so I threw my hat into the ring and was selected along with four others. Clyde Evans was the first to go. A true armor officer, he wanted to get out of the school environment as quickly as possible and through the obligatory two-year utilization assignment so he could get back to his tanks; USMLM needed two officers immediately and USARI released Clyde early for the assignment. By January of 1982, Clyde was in place. He was joined almost immediately by Paul Nelson. Around March, Nick Nicholson and John Eschrich were released early and also reported into USMLM.

As Clyde, Paul, Nick, and John relocated to West Berlin, I was riding trucks from Helsinki, Finland to Moscow, accompanying materials being trucked in for the construction of the new US Embassy in Moscow. Most foreign area officers follow up work on their graduate degree by spending one or two years in-country, honing their language skills and learning more about the culture in their areas of expertise. USARI was a substitute for this experience for Soviet FAOs. The Soviets were not particularly enthusiastic about allowing a bunch of US military officers onto the territory of the Soviet Union to hone their skills, so the Army tried to replicate the experience by setting up a Russian-oriented community in Garmisch. It wasn't a bad theory and worked to a degree. But the objective was always to try to gain language and cultural experience. So any opportunity to actually get into the Soviet Union was taken advantage of. For most of the students at USARI, this generally took the form of organized tourist trips throughout the Soviet Union and Eastern Europe. I participated in three or four of these trips with my class. But when the State Department requested reliable government employees to ride trucks in from Helsinki to Moscow, USARI volunteered to fill the requirement. I was one of those who volunteered and was selected. For the last four months of my assignment to USARI, I rode trucks along with a couple of other classmates (Dan Devlin and Todd Milton). John Eschrich and Phil Hockensmith were the first to ride just before John headed to Berlin.

All of the above is background. The motivations and details for each Army officer assigned to USMLM were different. But the selection process for each was similar. The heavy majority was handpicked from among students attending the US Army Russian Institute in Garmisch. Students in Garmisch were branch qualified officers at the basic levels of their service branch, and generally all graduates of the Defense Language Institute in Monterey. All had master's degrees in a National Security-related area of study. All were senior captains or majors. And all were volunteers.

Chapter 3
Rookie Year: Training

In my own mind, I divide the time that I spent at the Mission into four parts: my rookie, junior, and senior years and then my last year as operations officer. Each year was characterized by different understanding and capabilities on my part.

My rookie year was characterized by a tremendous learning curve on two levels. First, from my training as an infantry officer, I thought I knew something about the Soviet military. After all, they were clearly the main threat to the United States and NATO; and all of my training to be an infantry officer was to prepare me to understand and fight them. I quickly grasped that I understood generalities of the Soviet military, but I really knew very little of the details. I spent the first year at the Mission learning about the Soviet military. This was necessary to make my tours into East Germany productive. Second, I had to learn how to tour. I had to learn how to prepare for a tour. I had to learn the geography of East Germany, how to get around, how to get in and out of target areas. I had to learn the rules—written and unwritten. This was necessary to keep my driver and me from getting hurt. I had to learn how to use my equipment to good advantage. I had to learn the Mission reporting system and learn to discipline myself to get those reports written in a timely fashion. I'm sure that other officers progressed faster (and some slower), but it took a year before I felt like I really had my act together and was really productive.

I started my training at the Mission by attending a special vehicle recognition training school run by the British in the United Kingdom. It was four weeks of intense memorization. For a new trainee it was overwhelming with hundreds of combat, engineering, air defense, communications vehicles, helicopters, and combat aircraft to study and memorize. Often vehicles were very similar with very minor characteristics separating them from each other. The differences, though minor, were often very important as they often provided the clues into the evolving force structure of the Soviet forces. The training was slow at first, giving students the opportunity to study each vehicle and its variants in detail. But then things speeded up. Quick glimpses of vehicles, video tapes of vehicles passing by at thirty or forty miles an hour, small glimpses of a part of a vehicle through a wood line—all with the expectation that by the end of the course these short glimpses and quick looks would be sufficient to allow the trainee to accurately identify equipment. The majority of the students (as you might imagine) were British. The British non-commissioned officers in attendance, and headed for assignment to the British Military Liaison Mission in Berlin (BRIXMIS), turned the entire course into a massive competition only interrupted by periodic tea breaks. The British NCOs excelled at quickly spotting the minute details necessary to identify sometimes exotic hardware only rarely seen in the field.

John Eschrich (also a classmate and recent graduate of USARI) and I lived in a British Officers Club on the facility and learned to be British gentlemen (or American approximations). We did our best to hold up the American end, but honestly the Brit NCOs kicked our butts.

This was only the beginning. A portion of each day was dedicated to aircraft recognition (I hated aircraft). Even during training, I knew that the Missions divided their activities into ground targets, monitored by ground (Army/Marine) teams, and air targets monitored by air (Air Force/Marine) teams. Nevertheless, Mission liaison teams never knew exactly what opportunities would be presented, and you had to prepare for everything.

The class was composed of about twenty NCOs and officers from the British and French liaison missions. It gave us an opportunity to get to know some of our counterparts with whom we would work in Berlin and East Germany over the next three years. Most importantly, we met Captain Jeremy York, who would be the Chief of British Ground Operations for most of the next three years. There was one French officer, Lieutenant Guy Boucheau (formerly Captain of the French Army Boxing team), and a good friend for the next three years. The training session was the beginning of the camaraderie between the personnel of the three missions that was the cornerstone of probably the closest cooperation that you could find between British, French, and American forces in Europe.

In addition to the equipment recognition training, the Brits also included some training on how to conduct a tour, but there were significant differences between the British and US touring methods. It seems that at the close of World War II, and as the Allies were negotiating the post war arrangements, at least in the area of the role of the liaison between the residual military forces, the British better understood the potential future usefulness of the liaison missions than did the Americans. The Soviets negotiated separate liaison agreements between the British, French, American forces, and themselves. While the terms of the agreements were similar, the size of the missions was not. The British negotiated a mission (referred to by the British as BRIXMIS) to the Group of Soviet Forces, Germany, of forty-five members; the US negotiated a team of only fourteen.; the French negotiated a team of sixteen. As a result of their larger numbers, British tour teams were routinely composed of three members. Because of the smaller size, US tour teams were normally two members. So the techniques of the British were somewhat different than those used by USMLM simply by virtue of a third member on every team.

Detentions occurred on a regular basis to all of the Missions. There was common agreement to the approach between the three missions. Detentions occurred when a team was caught with no practical way to escape. There was no negative stigma associated with being caught; in fact, it was just the opposite. It was the responsibility of the officer on each team to recognize when the safest course of action was to simply give up and halt, surrendering to pursuing forces. Often detentions were high-tension situations. Teams attempted to avoid detention for two reasons. The histories of the missions were replete with situations in which efforts to halt teams were often conducted by ramming or blockading of vehicles. Teams were sometimes pulled from vehicles, roughed up, beaten up, tied up, equipment confiscated, etc. Shots were fired at Mission personnel frequently enough to be ever-present in the mind of a tour team. Soviet units clearly had instructions to take whatever measures necessary to capture teams without much guidance or limitation on what to do with teams after they halted them. Mission detention training focused on recognizing the imminence of a detention and appropriate steps to defuse tensions. Once it was clear that the team was captured and not attempting to escape, quick thinking by the senior tour member could often defuse the situation into an amicable discussion between the team and their captors.

The other problem of getting caught was that, once captured, local units did not have the authority to release the team. They were required to hold the team until the arrival of the local representative of the Kommandatura (somewhat equivalent to the Military Police in a US unit). The Kommandatura would conduct an investigation of the detention, detail it in writing along with some form of accusation against the liaison team and then demand that the detained team sign a form acknowledging their guilt. Teams routinely refused to sign and were subsequently released or escorted from the area. The whole episode could last from four to twenty-four hours, resulting in a substantial loss of time for the team. A good portion of our time at the British training course was focused on learning to manage detentions.

At the end of the equipment recognition course, I was anxious to get on the road in East Germany and put my new knowledge quickly to work before I started forgetting it.

· · ·

John Eschrich and I returned from our trip to Great Britain to our first exposure to how rough touring in East Germany could really be. Earlier, just before we left on our trip to Britain, there had been a very rough detention for one of our teams in the vicinity of a small Soviet garrison in southeastern East Germany. I visited this location many times in the following four years and was always struck by the absolute bad luck of this team. The observable portion of the installation was a small training area about two kilometers in length by half a kilometer wide. The training area was actually within a Permanent Restricted Area (PRA), but it was not necessary to penetrate the PRA to check the facility. The observation point was perfect from a tour team's perspective: nearly a kilometer away from the target, across a river on a seven hundred to eight hundred-foot high bluff. The only thing observable was a small driver's training course that was used to train new drivers how to operate their vehicles in varied terrain. It was only used a couple of times a year, as drivers' training was a cyclical event occurring in the spring and fall. In all of the times that I visited the site to check on it in following years, I never saw it in use by more than a couple of vehicles. It was a really low key, sleepy little place.

So, how did a tour team get detained on a high bluff a kilometer away from a sleepy little drivers training area? Well they approached the observation point from one of two normal approaches into the area to the edge of the wood line on the bluff. They checked out the edge of the wood line for the presence of any Soviet or East German military or police units and, seeing none, set up on the edge of the wood line to watch the facility for a few minutes. They weren't expecting to see much. The day was hot, and they had the vehicle top hatch open while they watched.

Unbeknownst to them, very nearby a Soviet Spetznaz (Spetzialnaya Naznacheniya) unit was conducting a small unit operations training exercise in the woods and had seen the tour team as they checked out the wood line. The Spetznaz are somewhat akin to US Army Rangers and probably the best of the Soviet ground forces. Spetzialnaya Naznacheniya means "Special Operations," and they were well-trained and dressed for what was to follow. Dressed in camouflage uniforms and seeing the vehicle, they immediately recognized it as a Mission tour vehicle. The entire unit dropped to the ground and hid. They waited until the vehicle came to a halt only a short distance away. They then stealthily approached the team until they were within just a few meters.

The US team may not have been as alert as they could have been in some circumstances—after all, they were a kilometer away from the target and had already checked out the immediate vicinity. When the Spetznaz unit launched itself at the tour vehicle it was too late. As the team tried to get the windows up, the driver was punched repeatedly in the face, yet managed to get the window up to a nearly-closed position. But as the tour officer attempted to close the roof hatch, two young Spetznaz soldiers leaped on top of the vehicle, kicked the hatch back open, and began kicking downward into the vehicle. The tour NCO was kicked nearly unconscious and the tour officer dragged from the vehicle through the top hatch by his hair. Out of the vehicle, the officer was then roughed up for another few minutes while being tied up with rope and duct tape. The NCO was also pulled from the vehicle and tied up.

The Spetznaz soldiers then proceeded to pull the team's equipment from the vehicle and drove the Gelande Wagon around the top of the hill for the next hour as they waited the arrival of the local Kommandatura.

There was no sympathy from the Kommandatura. They performed as usual, conducting an investigation, documenting their findings in writing, and then demanded that the tour officer sign the "Akt"—as they referred to the accusing document. Per Mission policy, the tour officer refused. They were allowed back into the vehicle and then escorted from the area. Much of the team's equipment was confiscated.

This had all occurred just before I went to the training in Britain. Any time a detention or an incident occurred to a US liaison team, Mission procedure was to conduct an internal debriefing including all of the tour teams not on the road. To the credit of the Mission leaders, this was not a witch-hunt or a crucifixion but a learning experience. The team involved in the incident was asked to describe the event as accurately as possible, and then, as a group, we took it apart to determine if it was just bad luck (it sometimes was) or if there were some lessons that could be learned. For me, I took one big lesson away from this event: no matter how safe you thought you were while on tour in East Germany, you were never really safe. I will admit that there were many times in the following years when I was pretty relaxed about a particular location or activity and let my guard down. But I never forgot this event. It made a big impression.

But this isn't the end of the story. The team had been treated pretty roughly, and they were pulled off of the road for about a month to allow them to calm down and get themselves back together. The description above is pretty antiseptic and does not really do justice to the violence of the encounter. The team was pretty shaken on their return.

A month or so later, the tour officer and NCO went back on the road while John and I were still in Britain. Just a few days before we returned, the tour officer was involved in a second and even more violent event.

Within what we called the "Local Area," a roughly one hundred-kilometer radius around Berlin, there were two Soviet Divisions—the 34th Guards Artillery Division, located very near USMLM's operating headquarter s in Potsdam, and the 35th Motorized Rifle Division, located primarily in Dallgow-Doeberitz (the old 1936 Olympic village), northwest of Berlin. Because of its close proximity to Berlin and the density of units in this area (the Headquarters of the Group of Soviet Forces, Germany, and a significant Soviet airfield were also contained in the local area), the three Allied Missions rotated coverage of the area on a daily basis. The units in this area got routine coverage by the missions and had better plans for dealing with Mission vehicles than any of the other units in East Germany. If they were active, we all knew that we had to be careful because they would be ready for any Mission vehicle they spotted.

One of the routine locations that the Missions monitored for activity was the military rail siding at Dallgow-Doeberitz. It was a tight place with only three or four monitoring spots. The Mission tour teams knew the spots and so did the personnel of the 35th MRD. When nothing was going on, the spots were pretty low key. When units were arriving or departing by rail, units would often post guards, roadblocks, or ambushes. The easiest of the checkpoints was at the west end of the loading ramp where a road crossed the rail line. Often, teams would simply run this road, check the ramp to see if activity was in progress, and, if so, they would not try to check the loading ramp any closer. We would just run down the rail-line several kilometers and wait for the train to depart or the next train to arrive. The only complication was that the trains could go west or north out of the rail yard and you had to make an educated guess or keep bouncing between the two rail lines to determine which line was being used.

It was a worst-case scenario. Mission tour team arriving, not yet aware that a load out was underway, and a local unit ready with an ambush waiting at the checkpoint at the west end of the loading ramp—the safest of the checkpoints. The tour team was ambushed by soldiers surrounding the railroad crossing point. The soldiers leaped out of hidden positions as the vehicle slowed in the middle of the rail crossing to look down the ramp. Before they could react, the soldiers were on them and the vehicle surrounded. Reacting instinctively, and with the last violent detention still fresh in his mind, the tour officer ordered the tour NCO to move out. As the vehicle began to move, a Soviet lieutenant leading the ambush leaped onto the hood of the vehicle and hung on. The team did not stop but progressed through the rest of the soldiers, at which point the lieutenant lost his grip and slid off the front of the vehicle and was run over. The tour team halted, and an ambulance arrived to take the lieutenant away (still alive at the time). The Kommandatura arrived to investigate the incident. Following refusals to sign the Akt, the team was escorted to Glienicke Bridge and allowed to return into West Berlin.

The consequences were harsh. It was apparent that if the US did not take action unilaterally, the team would be formally declared *persona non grata*

(PNG'd in Mission lingo). The US Mission voluntarily and officially withdrew the all of the team's accreditation as liaison personnel to GSFG HQ, and they were no longer allowed to tour into East Germany. The GSFG leadership demanded even stronger disciplinary action against the team members alleging variously that the Lieutenant had died, was seriously injured, was in the hospital for months, and so on. There was no doubt that he had suffered at least a serious injury. (The actual status of this lieutenant was never clear to me. We heard conflicting reports over the next year, but we could never tell when the Sovs were telling us the truth or just posturing.)

Our internal debrief focused on what could have prevented the incident from going as badly as it had. The key lesson that I carried away was that at the point that the lieutenant was on the vehicle further efforts to evade were dangerous to him and not justified. At that point, the team should have halted and accepted the detention. However, the situation was complicated by the very fresh memory of the tour officer's previous detention that had taken a very different and violent direction. It took me thirty minutes to write this somewhat detailed but leisurely dissection of an event that, for the tour team, happened in about five seconds. In real time, it was a tough call.

On a personal level, for this particular team, there was a brand new tour officer—a young Marine Captain, riding in the backseat of the vehicle on his very first tour; simply along for the ride to observe how an experienced tour team operated. His credentials were pulled along with the rest of the tour team through no fault of his own—just bad luck. He had only been at the Mission for about the same time that I had and was reassigned (as was the rest of the team) shortly thereafter. I took another lesson away from this event that stood me in good stead later. If you were in the car, you suffered the same consequences as everyone else in the car. You had a personal responsibility for the tour team's actions along with everyone else.

I felt very sorry for the young marine; he was a good officer and was disappointed to be removed from an assignment that he had been looking forward to. But on the positive side, his replacement was Marine Major Larry Kelley. Larry would be a key to many events that followed in my time as a liaison officer at the Mission, and a life-long friend as well.

• • •

Finally, I got my credentials as a liaison officer to the Group of Soviet Forces, Germany, and could quit just looking at pictures for equipment identification training. My very first tour would be with Paul Nelson, who had only been at the Mission for about four months longer than me but had already established himself as a solid performer. Paul referred to departing tour officer, Cole Gable, as his mentor. I took this to heart as a positive sign since there were a ton of "Cole Gable" stories floating around the Mission. Sergeant Randy Everett was our driver—one of the most experienced tour NCOs.

The approach by the Mission to training new tour officers (and NCOs) was to put the new guy in the back seat of the vehicle for about three tours with very experienced tour teams; then let the new tour officer be "in charge" for about two or three tours with an experienced tour officer riding in the back seat to help out (and take charge if things went really bad). Then the tour officer would be out on his own, but with a very experienced tour NCO. Targets for the first couple of solo missions would be pretty easy to cover and selected for their relatively low risk. Usually, at least one of the first two or three tours would be in the local area.

These first few tours flew by for me, but I will never forget parts of the very first trip. Every trip covered somewhere between eight hundred and 1500 kilometers. A lot of that was transit time on main roads or sneaking through back roads trying to get close to targets without being detected. I was on total "soak." I was trying to absorb everything—tour routes, approaches into targets, sneaking techniques, communications, and signals between the tour officer and NCO, positioning and use of equipment, on and on. Paul was really confident, and I was really relaxed. I had been around Paul for over four years now, and I knew that he knew what he was doing. Honestly, that first trip was incredibly fun.

I remember two events distinctly that I carried lessons away from. Every tour officer had his own techniques, and I learned some from Paul and began to develop my own.

We started south out of Potsdam on East German Route 2 down through the city of Wittenberg. Wittenberg held the cathedral at which Martin Luther had posted his dissention with the Catholic Church. Later, the Soviets would declare this city within one of their PRAs and close the city to Mission visits. But for now we drove south through the city with a quick swing past the cathedral. South and east of Wittenberg was an Engineer Training Area. Engineer units would deploy to the area for a week or so at a time from units of the 2nd Guards Tank Army (GTA). These units often had the latest Soviet engineering equipment, and the motor pool parking area was a prime target for good handheld photos. We poked around the outskirts of the training area for about thirty minutes, getting what we could without being seen.

Then Paul said, "Get ready. We're going to drive through the middle of the camp. I'll take pictures. Randy, you identify the equipment; and Tom, you get some of the Vehicle Registration Numbers" (VRN—equivalent to a license plate number).

It was still about 0700 in the morning, pretty good light, and the camp was coming to life. We turned into the main entrance into the camp and accelerated forward. The soldiers were all in formation for morning reveille with lieutenants out barking commands. We sped past the formation headed for the motor park. Paul had his camera up and the motor-drive running as fast as he could punch the button. His voice recorder was taped to the dashboard of the G-Wagon, and Randy was shouting out equipment identifications. I was overwhelmed with the speed of the action but started trying to read and shout out the VRNs from the license plates of all of the vehicles that I could see. I knew from my training that I was supposed to be trying to get the numbers from the same vehicles that Randy was identifying, but things were moving too fast, so I just got what I could.

It was all over in about one minute. Paul had shot up a whole thirty-six shot role-of-film that gave a good panorama of the motor park, and we had a good smattering of VRNs that would help identify the particular unit. We were out the back entrance of the training area and gone before the Sovs really had any chance to react.

Wow! Fast! Exciting! Big grins all around. Moving on and headed for the next target. My first major adrenalin high! We talked about it as we headed down the highway. Paul's approach was "pick their pocket" for all you could get without them seeing you. Then make one last run at them without worrying about being seen and grab as much information as you could. Then get out of dodge. Paul's philosophy was that you could sometimes get more detail in that last run than a couple hours-worth of "snooping." I pocketed this as a lesson learned. It made sense to me. I would learn to modify Paul's approach to fit my style as time went on.

The second event that I remember from that first trip occurred at what we referred to as the Southern Elbe River Training Site. All along the Elbe were tall dikes built to prevent flooding in the spring and early summer. Along the dikes were periodic breaks where roads or tactical trails cut through. When the floods came, only the breaks had to be sandbagged. By my judgment, it was a pretty efficient system. It had a big benefit for tour teams. When Soviet units were conducting river-crossing operations, the units were often located entirely inside the dikes, so you could get pretty close without being seen. Sometimes they put scout vehicles (BRDM-1 or BRDM-2s) on the dikes to keep watch, but often they did not.

We slipped up on the training site from outside the dike and then poked the nose of our vehicle through one of the breaks. We were lucky. There was a training exercise in progress. They were about a kilometer away, so we pushed on through the dike and moved behind some fairly sparsely-scattered trees trying to get fairly close to the training. We got to within about three or four hundred meters before we spotted an outlying recon vehicle (BRDM-2) about the same time he saw us. In a US liaison team, the NCO was not only the driver but also had primary responsibility for security. Randy saw the BRDM-2 crank up and immediately reversed course to head for the nearest break in the dike. The BRDM-2 started for the same entrance. Paul was busy with his camera and a telephoto lens, getting pictures of what he could. In the distance, I could see a PTS—a large, tracked, boat-like, amphibious vehicle used to ferry tanks and other vehicles across rivers also start up. It blew black smoke from its smokestack in big puffs and started ominously across the flat land to a second opening in the dike.

Randy had us moving fast. I didn't see why he was so worried as we were well in front of the BRDM-2 and the PTS looked too big and slow to be much of a threat. We hit the break in the dike and raced up to a ninety-degree turn in the road. A mile ahead was the main highway that, once we reached it, we were clearly out of danger. On the paved highway our G-Wagon could outrun any but the fastest of the Soviet vehicles (over time, I was to discover which vehicles were difficult to outrun). We were clearly outrunning the BRDM-2, and he did not look like he was working too hard to catch up—more as if he was just herding us forward. Then I could see why. As we made our ninety-degree turn toward the main road, the PTS broke through the dike. It didn't stick to the road but cut straight across the open field in an effort to cut us off.

Randy had us flying. I watched in amazement at the speed of the PTS. I couldn't believe that a tracked vehicle, that big, could travel so fast. He was trying to cut us off before we could get to the highway. Well, we beat him to the point at which he was trying to cut us off. As he pulled out of the field and up on the road to follow us to the highway, Paul yelled at me to take his picture. I did—about the only picture that I took on that trip. But I kept it through my entire tour at the Mission. He was so close that the picture showed the whole front of the PTS filling up the back window of the G-Wagon. It was my second lesson of the day: never underestimate the speed of a Soviet-tracked vehicle.

I really only remember one other trip from my training tours, and that more as a lesson of how big and complex a country we were operating in than anything special that occurred. I was back-seating with LTC Greg Govan, who, at the time, was the Chief of Ground Operations. I can't really comment on the professionalism of the Mission at other times, but I attribute the professionalism that I felt while I was there to LTC Govan and Major Mark Beto. Every mission assigned to a team was for a purpose that was clearly conveyed to the team. Preparation for every mission was expected to be professional. Thorough target folders allowing teams to prepare themselves were maintained to exacting standards. Reports were expected to be complete, accurate, and timely. Greg used to grade our reports. I was usually pleased except that he would never give me an A because my handwriting was so bad.

At any rate, I was back-seating with LTC Govan as we ran a column of towed artillery. I can still remember the vehicles, and today I can tell you they were towed T-12 anti-tank guns—a whole battery. But at the time I was lost. Here I was trying to make a good impression on my third tour on the road with the chief of ground operations in the car, and I couldn't even identify the simplest of anti-tank guns. For two years after that I tried to figure out where we had seen these guns, but for the life of me I couldn't figure it out. Then one day, nearly two years later, I was running down a road and recognized the spot. It was in what we called the "Luebben Triangle," a triangle of roads near the small town of Luebben, east-south-east of Berlin.

At any rate, I must have survived the event because I continued to tour. I learned that all of the tours conducted with a second officer in the vehicle were debriefed to the chief of ground and the ground operations officer. It made sense, and later when I became the Ground Operations Officer I saw the necessity of the requirement.

During this training period (and for my first year at USMLM), Colonel Randy Greenwalt was the Chief of Mission. COL Greenwalt liked to drop down in the basement of the Mission Headquarters (which is where the tour officers and NCOs were confined during the times that they were not on the road) and visit with the tour officers. It was his second tour at the Mission as he had been assigned once before as a tour officer himself, so he liked to drop in and share experiences. Most of it was the kind of things that colonels always say to captains and majors; but one piece of advice made big sense to me and stuck as a key part of my training. He said that every new officer or NCO began touring with a sense of where the threat was and when the team was potentially in danger. At the beginning on your first tours, you crossed the Glienicke Bridge into East Germany and immediately felt at risk. After a couple of tours, a new tour officer or NCO very quickly disabused themselves of this fear and began to narrow those areas in which they thought they were at risk, first to areas near garrisons and training activities, then to areas in the immediate vicinity of garrisons or training activities. As experience grew, those areas became smaller and smaller until, for some officers and NCOs, the fear went completely away. This was when you were in the greatest danger. As a tour officer, you had to put realistic bounds on your fears or you would never get close enough to gather any information of value. But you could never forget that there were places that you *should be* afraid because you were in real danger. This made sense to me and became a part of my tour officer milieu of operations.

I learned many other things from Paul Nelson—but one thing in particular. He said it on our first trip and many times afterwards: "As a tour officer, you have to constantly keep the odds in mind. At any given moment in East Germany, there were fourteen USMLM tour officers and NCOS, and 100,000 Soviet soldiers and officers. And they all have guns."

I guess my last thought on training was an event that occurred near the end of my training period. I had been assigned to the Mission for a total of about three months and had only conducted a few solo tours at the time. But LTC Govan called all of the tour officers together one afternoon and gave us all a sound lecture about poor performance, particularly in the area of accuracy of equipment identification in our reports and the quality of our reporting. It was pretty harsh and critical, but I didn't take it too much to heart personally. I hadn't been at the Mission long enough to make as many mistakes as he described. But I also knew that if I had been there longer I could be because we had no program to improve vehicle recognition skills except self-study. So after the lecture I went to him to bring this lack of a training program to his attention. I was instantly designated as the Ground Division Training Officer. I have to say, it was probably one of the best things that happened to me because I really had to teach myself to be an expert at equipment recognition in order to prepare the equipment recognition classes. I enjoyed it enough that I kept the position for over three years.

There was no formal graduation ceremony that said, Okay, you are now a full-fledged tour officer. You just began receiving tour assignments.

Chapter 4
Training: Rules and Tools

I finally got the back-seating and front-seating training sessions behind me and was on my own. Solo. Or actually a duo because you always had an NCO with you, driving and pulling the primary load for security. But I was through the "three-guys-in-the-car" routine which was crowded, and for certain meant that the third guy, the officer providing the training, was really in charge. After about a month of this, I was on my own.

I discovered two things immediately. First, despite the fact that I felt I was ready to be on the road on my own, preparing for a trip was more intense when there wasn't someone else there to turn to and make sure that you were doing things right. The process was simple and organized. You received your list of targets from the ground operations officer—in my case, from Major Mark Beto, who was already much of a legend at the Mission for some of his exploits and successes as a tour officer. The "target list" specified the targets to be hit and a short statement of the primary task at the target. It might be as simple as "look for recent or ongoing activity" or "photograph vehicles in the motor pool." Or it might be "obtain VRN from vehicles in installation" [VRN—Vehicle Registration Number] or "check training area for indications of beginning of driver training activities." The list would be accompanied by grid coordinates and target numbers linked to USMLM-specific target folders. The tour NCO that would accompany the officer would also be identified along with the start date and time, and anticipated return date for the tour.

If they were not provided with the target list, I would pull all of the target folders for the assigned targets. This was the critical step for both the security and success of the mission. Target folders were maintained by the mission for every known target in East Germany, including active targets, old targets—any place that any Soviet or East German military activity had been observed or suspected to have taken place. The target folders included a map of the area (1:50,000 scale) indicating the exact location. Then there were sketches by previous tour teams indicating the physical layout of the targeted facility or training area, also indicating other nearby facilities to facilitate the planning of routes into and out of the facility. The maps or accompanying text usually indicated best or safest routes into and out of the area. They indicated the reasons why teams had been targeted at the sites before (along with the dates) and what was found and where. There was always a page to indicate specific warnings about the site—incidents that had occurred, where the security was usually located, how the personnel at the site tended to react to Mission teams, anything that a new team might need to know to execute the task safely. For most targets there were included a number of photos of the key target areas to help tour officers visualize the target. For some low-key targets, the target folder might only contain three or four pages, or one of your mission tasks might be to conduct a recon to prepare the initial target folder. One of the key steps following every liaison tour was for the tour officer to update the target folder. Each officer indicated his name, the date of his tour, and the name of the NCO that accompanied him and added details and photos to assist follow-on tours. Hi-visibility targets might be two inches thick with records of coverage by numerous tour teams. The last entry in each folder would tell me who had been to the target most recently.

My next step (learned from others during my training sessions) was to pull each officer and NCO that had recently visited one of my targets aside and pump them for information. I would take the target folder, lay out the map and ask them show me the routes they used, in and out, situations they encountered—specifically the location of security personnel, and where they had encountered activity. The tour officer- and NCO-working areas in the windowless basement of the USMLM headquarters building in West Berlin were pretty small and close. Anytime you started asking questions about a specific location, everyone that knew anything about the target generally chimed in. You could learn a lot in a half-hour's discussion about one target. You couldn't neglect the inputs from the NCOs because they often knew more routes into and out of facilities than anyone else.

As a rule, the NCOs assigned as drivers on a tour were also required to check the target folders. They mostly looked to re-familiarize themselves with routes in and out and the security details. But the NCOs were on the road much more than the tour officers—about half again as often—so they sometimes skipped this because they felt they were pretty familiar with most of the real targets.

"Better do a thorough job, myself," I thought.

If I was tasked, for example, to get photographs of vehicles in the motor pool, I would ask others how they thought it was best to get at the motor pool, where I might encounter trouble, and how to get away if things went bad. This always started a hefty discussion between everyone who heard the question because different officers and NCOs had different approaches. Some were extremely aggressive and bold in their approach—which often led to an exciting departure at speed from the target. Others were more cautious seeking to get close without being seen and gathering information with less danger of aggressive reaction. There were trade-offs. More aggressive tactics were usually in broad daylight when photographic conditions were better but also when more soldiers and security were up and about and likely to react. More cautious tactics usually required approaches in periods of weaker daylight (or no light), seriously reducing photographic capabilities but occurring when Soviet or East German security might be reduced. Everyone had an opinion, and everyone had a story to tell. During two or three years at the Mission, you would likely hit nearly every target in East Germany at least once—some of the more important targets repeatedly. So I listened seriously to the older, more experienced tour officers and NCOs for their experience but gave weight to the opinions of anyone who had been to the target recently.

I would then come up with a tour plan for the entire target list. The targets were usually in clusters spread across USMLM's current sector of East Germany. If all targets were covered, most regular tours (other than the local) ran somewhere around eight hundred to 1500 kilometers. I would plot a general route, including how my team would travel to and between targets, where we would begin trying to shake our surveillance and exit the main roads, how we would approach a specific target area, in what sequence and how we would approach each target in a given area. Then I would walk myself through the tour, focusing on approach routes, target tasks, and egress routes from each target. I would walk through the entire route again with the assigned tour NCO and get his inputs. They often had recommendations for approach routes that saved time or avoided security choke points where surveillance units sometimes tried to pick up teams that had escaped their surveillance nets earlier.

None of this was original with me. It was a process that had evolved at the Mission over its forty-year history and had proven itself. The system worked. Nothing guaranteed that any plan would be executed exactly as put together or that security would be where it was supposed to be or that ingress and egress routes would be available as planned. But it reduced the operation to a process that gave high confidence to success while minimizing risk. It made sense to me so I followed the plan. The longer I toured, the less time preparations took but the steps never changed.

• • •

I guess one thing that was unique to me was that I was not good at remembering all of my targets. After a couple of rookie tours, in which I missed covering one or more of my targets or did not do everything requested at a target, I decided I needed a solution. Among the supplies available to liaison teams was water-soluble paper. So I made cryptic notes to myself on this paper and took it with me. Normally I kept the notes in the G-Wagon in my camera bag, always ready to dispose of them in a nearby Coke if needed. Only once did this bite me when I got caught in the 11th Guards Tank Division training area north of Dresden and was out of the car with my notes in my pocket. At an opportune moment, I ate my notes—not so tasty.

• • •

I mentioned that tours were assigned in the USMLM "sector." That's another thing that I had to learn. The three missions—USMLM, BRIXMIS, and FMLM—coordinated their efforts. All three missions were aware of where the main targets in East Germany were located. All knew which ones were the most important. So the probability that two missions might target the same facility on the same day was high unless they coordinated with each other. Why would this matter? Well, even in the times when coordination was close between them, it still happened that a team from one mission would "drop in" on a target (and there were reasons to do this, agreed among the missions), get the local unit all stirred up, and clear the area safely, only to be followed into the same target just a short time later by an unsuspecting tour team from another mission. Ambushes against an unsuspecting team by an already aroused installation or training-exercise security force was, in fact, the source of some of the worst incidents in Tri-Mission folklore.

In order to do what they could to avoid this circumstance the three missions coordinated their efforts. They divided East Germany into four sectors. The local (as I have mentioned earlier) was an area close about Berlin. There were a number of significant units in this area. Many military training exercises and rail movements transited the area because of the confluence of rail lines and a number of tactical trails used by armored units in and around Berlin. It was an area of intense interest to all three missions, so the area was defined and rotated by the three missions every twenty-four hours.

The remainder of East Germany was divided into three major sectors: A, B, and C. Sector A was generally defined as the area north of Berlin beginning with a line that ran due east of Berlin to the Polish border. It then circled Berlin counterclockwise north of the local to a line roughly to the north-northwest. Area B continued counter clockwise from this line to a line generally to the west-southwest of Berlin and the local sector. Area C was the remaining area located south and south east of Berlin and the local sector.

The area was further divided by designating every target in East Germany as either an "air target" or a "ground target." Air teams (generally manned by Air Force personnel in USMLM, occasionally supplemented by our resident Marine Corps pilot, Larry Kelley) covered the air targets and stayed away from ground targets. Ground teams (generally Army and Marine Corps personnel in USMLM) did just the opposite.

To ensure that each mission got maximum coverage throughout East Germany, the air teams rotated through the three sectors on a different cycle than the ground teams. So during any given moment, USMLM could have an air team in one sector and a ground team in another sector with a USMLM team in the local area (usually a ground team) every third day, leaving only one sector without coverage by a USMLM team. The missions coordinated the rotation between sectors at a specific date and time roughly every six weeks. Rotations occurred at midnight on the scheduled date. One of the most complex (and long distance) tours that a liaison team could be assigned began with a final wide sweep in one sector and then at midnight shifting to another sector to conduct an initial wide sweep of the new sector. In such a case it was not unusual for a team to begin its tour all the way to Rostock in the North in Sector A to be followed by a sweep clear to the West German border near the Fulda Gap in the southwest of Sector B—all in the course of forty-eight or fifty-four hours.

Except for the week following Nick's death, I do not remember a single day during the four years that I was at the Mission that there was not at least one USMLM team on the ground in East Germany; Christmas, New Years' Eve and Day, the fourth of July—all were workdays at the Mission.

• • •

Honestly, the first two or three months of touring for me were boring. It seemed to me that I was only getting about one trip per week and that, except for the local which was largely untargeted (because it was more of a patrol for activity rather than a targeting of specific installations), I was being assigned to very low interest, low activity targets. I was aware that the chief of Mission was about to be reassigned and was up for promotion to brigadier general. True or not, I suspected that new guys were being assigned to targets that would keep us out of trouble and USMLM out of the news. More senior guys were getting the more high-profile targets.

Actually, I could understand this because, being one of the new guys, I knew that my visit to a high-profile target was likely to be less productive than a visit by one of the experienced guys. But I didn't like it. How was I supposed to get better at touring and more productive if I didn't get the opportunity to test myself and grow?

So I complained to Mark Beto who, as Ground Operations Officer, controlled scheduling and targeting of tours. Mark took me at my word. I wasn't getting enough time on the road? He fixed that. It seemed to me that for the next six months I was on the road almost constantly. We had been tasked to check and catalog every known forest bivouac site and clump of trees capable of holding a bivouac site in all of East Germany, starting in the north near Rostock, and finishing on the Czech border in the south. I spent the next six months in more forests than the East German Forest Meisters did checking out bivouac sites. I didn't get just the biv sites, I also was assigned to any military installation in the general vicinity of the biv sites I was working. So at least I was not just driving down empty roads. Most of the Bivouac sites were empty, but many held bunkers that I explored. I learned how they were set up, how they were secured, how to tell from a distance if they were occupied (some were). If they were occupied by guards, I learned to assess the attitudes of the guards and, if it looked okay, to drive on into the site, give them some cigarettes and sandwiches, and talk to them for a while. Some were so lonely they would talk to anyone. Some were suspicious and cautious. They all took the cigarettes and sandwiches. It was a chance to practice my Russian a little bit and also to learn how to evaluate soldier's reactions. Most were unarmed, but occasionally they had weapons. If they had weapons, there was often evidence that they were engaging in casual target practice—something no US soldier would ever get away with while on a guard post. I pocketed that information for future reference. No one was counting every round of their ammunition when they returned to garrison from guard duty like we would do for our troops.

If there were no guards, I checked the bunker out thoroughly looking for anything that would indicate which units used it or anything that they may have left behind from their latest visit. Sometimes we would find bit of paper or notes scrawled on tables with Unit FPNs—five-digit field postal numbers that the Soviets routinely used to identify their units rather than by the actual unit name. Linking the FPNs with specific unit names was a USMLM specialty and, when successfully linked, substantially increased the value of intelligence details that we gathered.

• • •

Our NCOs were a special breed. They were primarily responsible for two things on the tour—operating the vehicle and team security. Team security was shared; when your neck was on the line, you never gave the responsibility for security away completely. Particularly as a team approached a site, or as you were lying in wait for a vehicle column to approach, both team members—officer and NCO—would be fully alert for security. But once the cameras came out and the actual intelligence collection began, it was difficult for the officer to do both. I'm not sure what other officers did other than what I observed during my training, but on my team, as soon as the collection began, I gave the NCO full responsibility for deciding if we needed to run. I told them not to wait or ask. If they thought it was time to go, it was time to go. I got to know all of the NCOs very well and they were a gutsy crew. They were more prone to wait to the last second to give us the last bit of collection than to run at first warning.

When I first arrived at the Mission, the NCOs were generally chosen from the nearby Berlin Brigade. The Mission staff would go to the Brigade with a requirement, and the Brigade would look for volunteers. Each NCO went through a training process similar to the officers except it was more oriented on the vehicle operation and a little less thorough on the vehicle recognition end. Driving skills were critical. It was one area of expertise that the NCO really had to have on arrival. We didn't have time to give them special training. The NCOs worked with each other to train on maintenance and operation of the Mercedes Gelande Wagons. But, back to driving skills, the driver either had it or he didn't. If the NCO did not demonstrate good (meaning fast, quick-witted, safe, and skillful) driving skills, he was returned to the Berlin Brigade without prejudice. The NCOs went through a training and evaluation process similar to that of officers: three or four trips in the back seat, three or four trips as a driver with an NCO in the back seat giving advice, and then, if he did well, he was on the road with an experienced tour officer.

Probably the trickiest thing that the NCOs had to pull off was running a Soviet vehicle column head-on. Some of these columns included hundreds of vehicles and could stretch for several kilometers in length. As we ran the column we would turn on a voice recorder, and the NCO was responsible for calling out the vehicle identification while the officer called out the vehicle registration number. All the while, the NCO had to keep our vehicle moving safely in the right lane, watch for any dangerous reactions from vehicles in the column, and look for escape routes off the road in the event that vehicles in the column began to react to our presence. For the tour officer, often the first clue that things were about to go bad was the NCO's silence. That meant that he had noticed something of concern, had stopped calling out vehicle identifications, and was aggressively looking for an escape route (sometimes accompanied by expletives). Although we did not start using video cameras until my last year at the Mission, one of the funniest (in hindsight) videos I ever saw was shot by a French Mission team as they sat on the side of the road watching a column of Soviet trucks roll past. You could hear the team calling out vehicle identifications and VRNs, when suddenly in the video screen you could see a truck break out of the column and head right for them. Vehicle ID and VRNs halted in a flicker of a second and turned to shouts of *Watch out! Back up! Turn around! Here he comes!* (all in French, of course) accompanied by a string of French profanities. It was funny because they escaped without a scratch. It would have been less funny had it turned out differently.

Most of the NCOs were reasonably good at vehicle ID, but not all of the NCOs were great. But some took the same pride in their vehicle recognition skills that the Brit NCOs did—particularly, SFC Hans Tiffany (Tiff), who also often helped out in the vehicle recognition training. But for me, vehicle recognition was secondary for the NCOs. If they weren't great at it, I was rapidly gaining confidence in my own recognition skills, and what I really wanted from them was good vehicle operation and security. For my money, those two skills were about three times as important as the vehicle ID skill.

High speed escapes and chases were a way of life at the Mission. Not every tour was an exercise in excitement. But in retrospect, I would guess that somewhere around forty percent of my 165 missions into East Germany involved at least one high-speed chase. An NCO could either handle the vehicle at speed or he couldn't. If they couldn't, they didn't last. It was no reflection on their professionalism as an NCO in their normal Military Occupation Specialty (MOS); it was simply a reflection on their natural driving skills which were critical to this job. Earlier in Mission history, NCOs were sent to a professional high-speed racing course run by Mercedes in West Germany. However, this training did not translate as well to the operation of Gelande Wagons, so it was halted sometime before I got to the Mission. Occasionally, Mission NCOs and officers were sent to a West Berlin Police training course for Evasive Driving. I got to go; it was great fun; particularly since there were some important applications for us. But that was the best that the NCOs got. Really, they either came with driving skills or they didn't make it.

Vehicle operation meant more than driving down the road. Chosen because of the similarity of their silhouette to the Soviet Military UAZ-469, the Mercedes Gelande Wagons themselves were highly modified. The lights were modified to allow various configurations. The brake lights could be turned off during a high speed chase to hide from pursuers the fact that we were slowing down to make a sudden turn, often causing them to shoot by a turn, giving us just the small edge that we needed to get away. The lights on one side of the vehicle could be turned off so that, in the distance and in the dark, the vehicle could appear to be a motorcycle. The rear lights could be completely turned off while the front lights remained lit, hiding all indications of our actions from a pursuer or from surveillance vehicles. A set of infrared spotlights were added inside the grill on the front of the vehicle and, with other lights out, could be activated from inside the vehicle, providing enhanced visibility when we were using night-vision devices.

The G-Wagon was equipped with a full-length skid plate that came in handy many times in rough terrain. A powerful winch was added to the front bumper. Winching was a way of life. We often joked that we all signed up for the Mission because we thought we were going to get to "wench" our way across East Germany. We were only off by one letter. A monster gas tank was added that held around one hundred liters of gas allowing us to travel for long distances without refueling (always amazing to those in pursuit). Naturally, we carried a bag of tools most important of which, to me, was a massive set of bolt cutters used to cut our way through fences and gates. The G-Wagons were painted the standard ugly OD green of all US military vehicles of the time (ugly because it seemed a travesty to paint a Mercedes OD green) and equipped with special license plates that identified the vehicle as belonging to the US Military Liaison Mission. There were no weapons on board, no armor plating, no bullet-proof glass, and no communications equipment other than a standard AM/FM radio.

The NCOs had to know the vehicle inside and out. If a breakdown occurred, the NCO either fixed it on the spot (we carried a bag of basic spare parts) or he hiked to the nearest farm house to call back to the Mission for rescue. Navigating and winching was the officer's responsibility. If the officer navigated the vehicle into a mud hole, he had to get out, set the winch up, and oversee the winching. If there were no trees or other fixed objects nearby, we carried a "dead-man"—a large metal rail that was pinned to the ground with long stakes using a sledge hammer. The winch was then attached to the dead-man. "Winching out" was never one of my favorite activities. It always seemed to happen at the most inopportune moments.

We often operated the vehicles at night using night-vision goggles, but not the latest versions that the Army had. Because periodically a team was detained and all of the team's equipment was confiscated, we were not allowed to carry anything with leading-edge technology that might possibly fall into the hands of the best reverse-engineering experts in the world. I laughed when I read through the instruction manual for our night-vision goggles as it recommended that vehicles not be operated at greater than thirty kilometers per hour while wearing the goggles. It was not unusual for a tour team being followed by an East German surveillance team at night to accelerate to higher speeds (eighty plus mph) to gain some separation, put on the night-vision goggles, kill all of the vehicle lights, and then execute a sharp turn off the main road onto a side road or into a field under the cover of darkness—effectively "disappearing" from the field of view of the surveillance team. Despite these excesses, I don't know of any accident that ever occurred involving a Mission vehicle (from any of the Missions) while using night-vision devices—a tribute to the operating skills of our NCOs.

The NCOs pulled off escapes and driving feats that constantly amazed me. One afternoon I was with Jesse Schatz. We were checking out a small East German facility that seemed to be very sensitive and was quite difficult to approach as there was a long, very narrow driveway of about 300 meters with eight-foot walls on each side. The driveway followed a fairly steep decent until it opened up into a small training area with two or three buildings at the bottom end. We approached slowly down the driveway, and all seemed quiet. I had my camera ready to go into action as soon as we saw anything that might give a clue to the nature of the facility. At the end of the driveway (where the wall on the right side stopped and the training area began to open up before us), there were a number of head-high bushes on the right side of the drive. It was mid-afternoon on a sunny day, and we had the windows down to bring in the cool air and to allow us to hear any indications of vehicles running. Jesse halted the G-Wagon as we hit the opening into the training area to give us a quick look before we proceeded further. It was a little bit nerve-racking to be in an area that seemed to have only one exit.

As we checked out the area, I glanced to my right and saw an East German soldier hiding in the bushes only ten meters away.

I yelled, "Jesse, guard!"

Jesse slammed the G-Wagon into reverse and began backing up the driveway (no room to turn around) as an East German UAZ-469 (similar in size and shape to our G-Wagon) pulled into the driveway to pursue us up the hill. It was clear that they had hoped we would pull fully into the training area so that they could block our exit with the UAZ. Jesse's decision to halt at the entrance and my noticing the guard had foiled their plan. The UAZ followed us up the driveway, nose-to-nose with our backing G-Wagon. He stayed no more than twelve inches off our bumper for the entire three hundred meters. I couldn't see how Jesse was going to get us clear so that we could get turned around without the UAZ gaining the advantage and blocking us as we turned. But at the last minute Jesse let off the gas and slowed, causing the UAZ to bump our front bumper and to instinctively slow down. Then Jesse suddenly accelerated, giving us just enough space to turn sideways as we hit the main street, blocking the UAZ's access to the street while orienting the G-Wagon for rapid access to the road. In fact, the UAZ bumped the side of our vehicle as Jesse accelerated away, but once on the main road it was clear that we were going to get away and the UAZ halted pursuit. Great driving.

Later, I was with SGT Steve Eairheart as we drove down a two-lane paved road east of Erfurt. There was a major Soviet exercise in progress and we were trying to get ahead of several columns of rapidly-moving armored vehicles. We raced down the two-lane road and rounded a corner to encounter a roadblock of armored military vehicles and armed guards across both lanes of the road. They were no more than one hundred meters in front of us when we rounded the corner. Steve saw the roadblock, slammed on the brakes, and executed a high-speed reverse turn. The whole thing could not have taken more than ten seconds, and we were safely gone. Great driving.

All of the NCOs also spoke German most excellently. So we had someone in the vehicle that spoke Russian for close encounters with the Sovs, and someone who spoke German for interaction with local citizens and occasional interaction with East German soldiers. Often, East German local nationals, unhappy with the occupation of East Germany by Soviet military units, would recognize our vehicles, flag us down, and direct us to nearby Soviet military activities.

The NCOs spent more time on the road than the officers. This was primarily due to the requirement that the officer prepare extensive reports on observations obtained during a tour. So while the officer might be on a forty-eight-hour tour and return for forty-eight or seventy-two hours of report writing, the NCO would be on the road again in not less than twenty-four to forty-eight hours. As a result, during one year the average NCO might tour as much as thirty percent more than the average officer at the Mission.

Later, we began getting our drivers from a local Special Forces unit. This provided a smaller pool of NCOs to choose from, but all highly-motivated and professional. If there was a downside to getting NCOs from the Special Forces it was that they had no fear. Being chased or shot at by a single, upset Soviet soldier or vehicle was nothing in comparison with many of the things that they had experienced. On the upside, they were really cool in the tensest of situations.

I learned to be careful about what you trusted the NCOs with. They loved to pick up your camera while you were out of the car and snap a few shots off of you while you were investigating a bunker or climbing a tree to look over a fence. Some of those shots could get embarrassing, and you would not know about them until your film was developed the morning after the tour was completed—and after everyone in the photo lab had already seen them. But as a rule the NCOs were a pretty tight-lipped group. I know that tour officers periodically bent the rules or cut corners. Little comments occasionally from an NCO let you know that there was an "easier" way to approach a target or to move from one area to another that he had learned from one of the other tour officers. But they were very reluctant to name names or go into details of how they had learned the "easier" way. What happened on the road, stayed on the road—even within the brotherhood.

• • •

I have mentioned that by the terms of the Huebner-Malinin Agreement, the agreement establishing the US Military Liaison Mission, USMLM was authorized fourteen sets of credentials. Of this fourteen, one was always assigned to the chief of Mission, one was always assigned to the "house father," the officer or NCO assigned with full time responsibilities for managing the USMLM Potsdam House or the official headquarters of the Mission in Potsdam. The remainder of the US passes were split between the USMLM air and ground teams, usually five to the air team and seven to the ground team. But we actually had about forty or fifty percent more tour officers and NCOs than we had passes at any one time. So our routine was to keep officers and NCOs in an active liaison status for about six weeks at a time and then to withdraw their credentials and issue them to fresh personnel. The officer or NCO whose credentials were withdrawn was usually off the road for about four or five weeks, allowing them to rest up and to complete unfinished intelligence reports. Initially, this really bothered me. I felt like the longer I was on the road, the better I got at what I was doing. I loved the fulfillment of preparing and completing missions and the adrenalin rushes of close calls. I hated being pulled off the road. Even though I might have been on the road for six or seven weeks and averaged two tours of four to five days per week on the road, I thought I was still fresh and going strong. I was wrong. I started watching myself and others around me. Frankly, by the sixth week, tour officers and NCOs were not fresh. Six weeks of four or five days per week on the road with very little sleep was wearing. By the sixth week we were all running mostly on adrenalin. In my opinion, close calls came more frequently at the end of a tour period. Later, when I became the Ground Operations Officer, I began watching this very closely and it was readily apparent that people pushed themselves hard during tours and around six weeks was enough. Longer and the negative effects became readily apparent.

· · ·

Learning how to use my equipment was another challenge of my first year. Each officer was issued five (yes, five) Nikon F-3 titanium body cameras with a range of lenses. Every camera had a motor drive and could reel off a whole roll of thirty-six shots in just a few seconds. We carried powerful binoculars and spotting scopes and night-vision devices for both vision at night and as attachments to cameras. We carried multiple cameras for ease of rapid access. Day and night, I always had one camera either in my lap or on the floor between my feet. At night, it was equipped with a night-vision device. In the daytime, it had a thirty-five to 105mm zoom lens. I had a leather bag set up with wooden dividers within easy reach that contained two cameras equipped with large lenses (250mm, 500mm), one camera with another larger zoom lens, and one camera with color film. The bag also included a pocket camera (Canon Sureshot) for when I was out of the vehicle and wanted a small camera in my pocket. There was an assortment of other lenses ranging from wide angle (28mm) to telephoto (1000mm), a doubler and tripler (which doubled and tripled the power of lenses), and two powerful flash attachments.

Each liaison officer carried as much film as he thought necessary for any mission. I always carried at least fifty rolls, and I think I was about average. We used eight hundred ASA black-and-white film that seemed to work well with the broadest range of lenses and lighting situations. The film was often "pushed" for exposure to a maximum of 6400 ASA. It was grainy but provided some detail in bad lighting situations. We generally used black and white film because the recoverable detail was better than with color film. The color film was reserved for a situation in which color was necessary to see a particular feature of a target. One camera in my bag always had color film loaded.

Before I got to the Mission, and actually for most of the time that I was there, photography was one of my favorite hobbies. I had three cameras of my own, and, as my wife and I vacationed around Europe, I took dozens and dozens of rolls of film. But, by the time I had completed my tour at the Mission, photography had become work. I think I was good at it. I understood depth of field and aperture settings and film speeds and focal lengths. I knew which equipment combinations and film settings fit virtually every situation. I took good photos. But it stopped being fun. The camera became a tool that needed to be cared for and used properly in order to complete my work.

We carried 1:50,000 scale maps specially prepared by our NCOs to span the width of East Germany. The maps were annotated to indicate Permanent Restricted Areas (PRA). They were glued together and folded to allow you to track movement efficiently, east to west, by simply unfolding the map section-by-section. It took a series of about ten maps (all carefully labeled) to cover all of East Germany. When working in one sector (A, B, or C), you usually needed about four or five map series. We maintained about four or five copies of each map, and tour officers pulled the maps they needed for each tour based on the areas that they would be working. One of my rookie year lessons learned was that you always needed to carry all of the maps for the sector in which you would be working, not just the ones near your targets. A couple of times I got caught running off of the edge of my 1:50,000 map chasing an unexpected Soviet column trying to navigate using my 1:250,000 PRA map—not fun.

Every officer carried an official 1:250,000 scale map showing all of the Permanently Restricted Areas in East Germany (a single map showing all of East Germany and all of the PRAs on one map. Whenever a tour got caught, the first Soviet allegation was always that you were in a restricted area and the official map came out to help argue that we were not. Three times during my four-year term at the Mission, the Soviets issued new PRA maps. Each time, they provided each Mission (US, French, and British) with several copies. Each copy of the Soviet map was hand drawn so there were always variations between them. Each Mission turned their maps over to the British, who then produced an "official" version for all three Missions that took advantage of the most lenient of the Soviet versions provided. When the Soviets wanted to argue about a specific boundary indicated on our official map, the appropriate "official" map was produced to argue our case. Copies of the official map were distributed to every tour officer. Each time the Soviets distributed a new PRA map, it was done with no advance notice and effective immediately. Producing the new official maps was a high priority and was completed within days of being issued by the Soviets.

In addition to the official bag of camera equipment, every tour officer carried other equipment that seemed to come in handy from time to time. I carried a 500,000-candle-power spotlight, a handheld infrared spotlight, two flashlights (one small enough to fit in my pocket), a pry bar, a compass that I taped to the vehicle windshield for easy viewing, and heavy-duty gloves.

Referring to the 500,000 candle power spotlight brings to mind a couple of lessons that I learned during my rookie year that stood me in good stead throughout my tour with USMLM. One of the unusual circumstances that provided the gray area in which the Missions operated was that we were a remnant of the occupational period of the end of World War II. The agreements that allowed us to operate were signed by the occupying forces. The United States Government continued to view East Germany as an occupied area, not as a nation. The US did not have an Embassy in East Germany (in fact there was another "Mission" that represented the US Government to the East German authorities). As a result, the Missions did not recognize the authority of the East German Volkespolizei or military forces over our activities. We would not stop at their direction and routinely ignored them if they got in the way of our collection activities. This extended particularly to the East German Secret Police, or "Stasi," as the locals called them. But there was a practical side to everything as I discovered and learned to respect.

The Volkespolizei were as close to normal police officers as existed in East Germany. They controlled traffic, investigated accidents, broke up fights, etc. They also had a responsibility to report any Mission vehicles that they encountered up their chain of command. They were a part of an enormous effort by the East German authorities to keep track of the Mission teams. As long as the VP were on foot, they were rarely a problem to us as we just ignored them and went on. We tried to avoid them as much as possible as we approached targets because we knew that they would report our movement. But in a normal transit situation, we just ignored them.

But if they were in a vehicle they seemed to feel obligated to follow us. They usually were in Lada sedans (East European version of the Fiat) or Wartburgs and could not really keep up with us on the open road. But they were a hindrance. I finally decided to test a personal theory and began having my NCO slow down until they were close enough to our vehicle to clearly see our license plate. Our plates were numbered, so they would pursue us until they could the vehicle license plate number (no more than two digits—thirty-three, for example). In most cases, I discovered that as soon as they had the number they dropped off and went back to their normal area of responsibility. Occasionally, when we were having difficulty with surveillance and I did not want them to get our number and to feed it back to the surveillance teams, I would have the driver just race away and let them try to keep up. But they could be pretty persistent. Sometimes, even when we let them get close enough to get the vehicle number, they would continue to pursue and, even more irritating to me, they would get as close as they could and then turn their bright headlights on. I would tolerate that for a while thinking that maybe they were still trying to get the vehicle number. But after a reasonable amount of time, out came the 500,000-candle-power spotlight. It was amazing how fast a Volkspolizei vehicle would back off when you hit the driver right in the eyes with 500,000 candle power. I would leave it on until they backed off far enough for us to easily blow them off.

But in most cases, they were just doing their job, and I tried not to provoke them. One night, on the autobahn between Dresden and Leipzig, I was with Smitty (SGT Charles Smith). We had been going strong for over twenty-four hours and I was pretty tired. We were simply transiting the area, and I drifted off to sleep (not tolerated by the NCOs very often, but I learned to sleep with my head straight up and in the daytime with my sunglasses on, and caught a few winks here and there). Suddenly, I was startled awake by a tremendous crash. I opened my eyes to the sight of a small trailer sliding across the top of the hood of the car and the sound of Smitty cursing like a sailor. We had rammed the backend of a small Lada station wagon pulling a small trailer. Fortunately, no one was hurt, and when I got him calmed down Smitty told me what happened. It was around 0200 in the morning with no one else on the road. We were traveling pretty fast (one hundred kilometers per hour [KPH] or so) and came up quickly on the other vehicle that was only traveling about forty KPH in the left lane of the autobahn. As we approached, Smitty flipped the headlights several times, but the sedan remained in the left lane, so he shifted to the right lane to pass. Apparently startled by our headlights, at the last minute the sedan driver suddenly shifted to the right lane just as we started to pass. Wham. Fortunately, no one was hurt, but, unfortunately, the collision drove the tongue of the trailer into the back of the sedan and crushed our radiator. We were both crippled. Complicating things further, the driver of the sedan was inebriated.

It was bad luck for us because we were in a PRA. By the agreed rules of engagement, Mission vehicles were allowed to transit PRAs via the autobahns as long as we did not stop. So, we could not walk to a farm house or anywhere else to try to call for help. We just had to wait. The driver of the sedan and his daughter had blankets in the car, and I had a sleeping bag with me. Smitty had decided that he didn't need his sleeping bag for this trip even though I warned him before we left Potsdam. I let him suffer (he never left his sleeping bag behind again). He spent the night nursing a squad stove that was nearly out of gas trying to stay warm. Finally, around 0500, a Volkespolizei van pulled up with three officers inside. They had been called by one of the two or three vehicles that had passed the accident site (irritatingly, without stopping) during the night. I will compliment them. They were totally professional. USMLM personnel were not authorized to sign any East German documentation of any type, and I told them that I would not sign any papers. But I told them that Smitty and I would cooperate in their investigation by telling them what happened. They documented our story, showed it to us to be sure that they had it right, and then did not ask for signatures. They did not want to offer us assistance but agreed to call our duty officer at the Potsdam House to tell him of our situation and location. I was skeptical, but about three hours later, another USMLM G-Wagon appeared to tow us back to Berlin. They did their job.

Another story about the Volkespolizei from Mission lore was that a British team was running along an autobahn on a foggy morning when a VP vehicle pulled up beside them and began signaling them to pull over. The Brits took their disdain for the Volkespolizei almost to an art form and carried signs in their vehicle in German that they held up as appropriate to wave to the VP such as "BRIXMIS personnel are not subject to East German Authorities." The team waved signs, the VP gave up, and the BRIXMIS team drove off a steep embankment when the damaged autobahn suddenly ended. Maybe it was just a story, but it was part of what affected my thinking. Sometimes you needed to understand actions in context.

The Stasis are another story entirely, but I'll get to them later.

• • •

In addition to the maps with Permanent Restricted Areas, the Soviets tried to control liaison teams with two other devices: notices of Temporary Restricted Areas and Mission Restriction signs.

As a part of their planning for major exercises, someone on the staff of GSFG was responsible for issuing notices of Temporary Restricted Areas (TRA). It must have been a checkbox on their planning checklists because sometimes they were effective and sometimes not. We respected the notices because the US forces in West Germany also issued TRA notices to keep the Soviet Military Liaison Mission from sending teams in to observe US training exercises. But the Soviets were not always effective. TRA notices always had a specific start and end date and time. But sometimes, after a TRA notice was issued, exercise dates would slip and the TRA notice would not be adjusted. So not only did the TRA notice not keep us out, it actually pointed us to key areas. Until the very minute that a TRA began and immediately upon its expiration, Mission teams would be in the areas of the TRAs trying to detect early arrivals into the area or late departures. Particularly, we often caught remnants of units still in training areas and at rail sidings still loading out. If the planning was really bad, the TRA would lift while the exercise was still in progress.

To this day, I still do not understand the Soviet logic behind Mission Restriction signs. All over East Germany, around every installation, training site, or other areas of interest were signs announcing that "The Passage of Members of Military Liaison Missions Is Prohibited" in four languages. There was no written or unwritten agreement between the Allied Missions and GSFG to respect these signs or their prohibition. In fact, they were like magnets. New signs observed in an area attracted immediate attention. There were thousands of them. There must have been a factory that did nothing but produce MRS. One thing was sure. The Soviets and East German military units took them seriously, and we considered going "behind signs" to immediately increase our risk level.

If nothing else, MRS made great souvenirs. I suspect that nearly every liaison officer and NCO from every Allied Mission still has an MRS hanging in their garage or basement.

• • •

The most important lesson that I learned during my rookie year was not on the road but back at the Mission headquarters. Successful touring required serious preparation and was challenging in execution. But it wasn't over until the reporting was done.

Our reporting process was thorough, as was everything else about the Mission. There were three parts. Because of our relatively close proximity to the Glienicke Bridge, which all Missions used to enter and exit East Germany from West Berlin, all teams—even the British and French teams—stopped by the US Military Liaison Mission headquarters in West Berlin to complete what we called a mission "highlight." It is not exciting to write about mission reports, but, like many activities, the paperwork was the final step in completing a task. It was so important at the Mission that I will spend an entire chapter on it later.

Havel Parade

Not everything was intense and hostile. Sometimes things just happened and it was easier not to fight it but to just go with the flow. What do I mean by that? Well, let me give you an example. One early morning I was with Jesse Schatz and we were working the northern Elbe River crossing sites. There was almost always something going on at the northern Elbe sites, so I liked being there. We had arrived at first light and checked some of the bivouac sites. They had been recently used, but no one was there at the time. We were transiting from one area to another driving along the river dikes. There was a good road on top of the dike, and it gave us good visibility into the biv sites as we drove. But the dike we were on was not one that either Jesse or I were familiar with, and it led directly into the town of Havel. It was about 1000 and we decided to follow the dike road into Havel to an excellent bakery that Jesse knew about and that I wanted to put on my tour officer's list of places of special interest. As we turned onto the main street in Havel from the dike road it was filled with people and vehicles festively decorated. It appeared that we had turned onto the main route for a local celebration of some kind, and that we had just turned onto the main parade route. No one seemed particularly disturbed at our presence so I just shrugged and told Jesse not to do anything radical to get free of the parade. Seeing that the crowd seemed favorably disposed toward us, I stood up through the G-Wagons' sunroof and waved like a beauty queen. The crowd loved it. There we were in our US Military uniforms riding in an OD Green Gelande Wagon with US vehicle plates covered with US Flags. I think that had there been awards that day, we might have gotten the award for most popular. As it was, we stayed with the parade for the length of the main street and then left the parade at the far end of town. I still don't know what the mission protocol for joining parades is, so I discreetly left it out of my mission highlight report when we returned to Berlin later that day. We never got to the bakery.

Chapter 5

Rookie Year: Surveillance

I've often wondered if there was a security school in or near Potsdam that taught mobile surveillance techniques to East German Security personnel. The intelligence gathered by Mission personnel for the most part was basic order of battle information—the stuff that, if the Soviets had an equivalent of the US Military "Stars and Stripes" newspaper—would be commonly available. Yes, periodically we got highly technical information that had a higher significance, but most of it was pretty basic. What made it valuable was that it was not easily available and that what we obtained and reported was from a very reliable source—US military officers. But overall, it was pretty basic stuff.

But from the level of surveillance allotted to mission teams by the East Germans, you would think it was a lot more. I quickly learned that one of the very first things you had to do before you went in on a target was to blow any surveillance off. The Stasi, as the East Germans called them, were persistent and pervasive. Even on a slow day when virtually nothing was happening, it was very likely that one or more surveillance teams would be hanging around. We routinely started tours at varying hours so that it would be difficult to help the Stasi establish any kind of schedule for their personnel. Most USMLM tours started late at night or before dawn. We had a decided advantage in the dark. But each tour started by crossing the Glienicke Bridge on the southwest corner of West Berlin through a Soviet Checkpoint into Potsdam. I would guess that seventy to eighty percent of our teams then went directly to the USMLM Mission House in Potsdam before actually launching on a tour. At the house we would stock up on sandwiches, fruit, cokes, coffee, and other supplies prepared by the East German house staff, sufficient to carry us for two or three days, plus a bag full to pass out to Russian soldiers should the opportunity arise.

This stop off at the house gave the Stasi about one to two hours to get a team together to pick us up as we left the Potsdam House on our tour.

• • •

Let me digress to the Potsdam House for a few lines. The official headquarters of the US Military Liaison Mission to the Group of Soviet Forces, Germany, was the Mission House in Potsdam, East Germany. When we hosted a special event to which the Soviet military officials were invited, it was to the Mission House. When the Commander of US Army Europe (USAREUR) wanted to host a meeting with the Commander or staff of GSFG, the Mission House was a natural venue. USMLM's official function was liaison between US-AREUR and GSFG. All official communications from the GSFG Headquarters were delivered to the Mission House. For some years, tour officers and NCOs lived in small houses along the street leading into the Mission House. The house was supported by an East German staff that was paid by the Soviet External Relations Branch (SERB) from the GSFG Headquarters. As you might imagine, the East German Staff was tasked by GSFG to monitor and report the activities of USMLM personnel. The house was seriously bugged, and we made no attempt to debug. We just all knew and acted accordingly.

The House was manned twenty-four hours a day, seven days per week by either a USMLM officer or NCO. Normally an officer was assigned full-time responsibility for managing the operations of the House, although periodically an NCO bore the task. We all called whoever was responsible the "House Father." This was a full-time job for the House Father, and, of course in order to travel to East Germany, he had to have one of our fourteen authorized passes. The House Father spent all week at the House managing the staff, keeping it stocked with supplies, making sure that USMLM tours passing through were well cared for, and serving as the main conduit for most of our communications with SERB. On the weekends and holidays the House Father got a break and returned to West Berlin while one of the other officers or NCOs with a pass spelled him. While you were at the House, the East German Staff served all meals and would prepare to your request so House duty could actually be a treat if you took it that way. John Eschrich and his family really took it to heart and volunteered for House Duty on Christmas Eve for at least two of the three years that he was assigned (I know for sure about two because I had the local duty on two Christmas Eves and had dinner with his family).

The House was bugged and we all knew it. One of the funniest evidences of House-bugging occurred during my third year at the Mission (I know this is out of order but I'm talking about the House here). The House was undergoing a very serious renovation and was totally torn up on the inside. The House Father and the East German staff were operating out of a smaller, caretaker's house that was also on the property. Jesse Schatz was pulling House Duty, and I was the officer on call if anything came up. Jesse called me about 8:30 p.m. to say that two guys swam across the lake and had come onto the property, seeking asylum. It was a common misperception among the local East German populace that, because USMLM vehicles constantly entered the property and because we flew an American flag out front, the property had the same status as an Embassy. We did not have that status, but, nevertheless, periodically someone would come onto the property asking for asylum. As there was an East German guard at the front gate and the House was surrounded by other non-US properties, the Stasi knew almost immediately of such an event. Our standard operating procedure was to do what we could to assist asylum seekers to leave the property safely, but really there was little that we could do.

Jesse told me that he had informed the asylum seekers that we could not help them and that they would have to leave. But he told me that he thought that they had gone into the big house and were hiding there. Colonel LaJoie, the Mission Chief, was on leave so I called Lieutenant Colonel Larry Shofner, the Deputy, and told him what was going on. He told me he would meet me at the Mission Headquarters in Berlin and that we would drive out to the House. We picked up one of the Mercedes 350 sedans and drove to the house, arriving around 10:00 p.m. Jesse told us that he thought the two asylum seekers were still in the house.

We started searching the House and found them hiding in the attic. It was a depressing situation. We knew that we couldn't help them, and they knew there was no way out without the Stasi knowing and probably catching them. They begged us to take their names to pass to one of the human rights groups in the US that monitored such things, and Colonel Shofner took their names.

One of the complications for the asylum seekers to get off the property without being seen was that the House was completely surrounded by security/decorative floodlights that lit up the outside of the House and also allowed monitoring of access and egress to and from the House. We told the asylum seekers that we would turn out the lights for thirty minutes to give them a chance to get off the property in the dark. A complication arose. Because of the construction in the house we could not get to the circuit breakers to turn the lights off. But we didn't give up. The lights were mostly on the front of the house, away from the lake. So I started on one side of the house moving from floodlight to floodlight flipping them so that they faced away from the house. As I moved from light to light, I could hear people rushing away from the chain-link fence and bushes that surrounded the house. So I began moving faster and faster to flip lights as quickly as I could. There must have been at least twenty people hiding in the bushes that I could hear rushing away as I flipped the lights outward.

That's not the end of the story. Colonel Shofner, Jesse, and I went back to the caretaker's house to wait for the agreed thirty minutes. While we were there, a Soviet UAZ-469 arrived with two officers from SERB. They came to the door of the caretaker's house and told Col Shofner that they were under the impression that we were having a problem.

Colonel Shofner calmly noted that we had not called them with a problem and casually asked what had brought them to the Potsdam House. Then he bluntly asked them if they were monitoring our phone calls or our conversations within the house. Both officers became quite flustered and turned and left without pursuing the conversation further.

I don't know what happened to the asylum seekers. After thirty minutes, I went back out and returned the floodlights to their normal position, and Colonel Shofner and I left. Jesse maintained later that he thought the asylum seekers had gone back into the lake to swim back to the other side. Colonel Shofner passed their names to the human rights organization as requested, and that's the last we heard.

• • •

Back to surveillance. We all called getting rid of surveillance "de-Narc'ing." The Stasi surveillance effort was like a police narcotics surveillance operation, I guess; so that is where we got it.

It was amazing to me. You could almost count on having surveillance. You might think it was not there, but when you started looking for it they almost always were. Sometimes it was small scale—one to three cars. Sometimes it was large scale. One time I counted thirteen vehicles involved in the surveillance operation. Some of us speculated about there being a school for Stasi surveillance teams in Potsdam because sometimes there was lots of surveillance for no apparent reason. If it was a surveillance school, we were the perfect "rabbits." Between the three missions there were normally two to four tours teams departing daily and nightly.

Another reason that I thought it might be a school was that sometimes the surveillance was pretty good and sometimes it was awful (meaning poorly executed). We had two advantages over the surveillance. As a rule, our G-Wagons were faster than the Ladas that they normally used. And once it got dark our night-vision equipment let us operate in darkness while they required lights. We also knew where we were going, and they were just guessing; so that also gave us an edge.

They often made it easy. There were always two or three big guys in the car, sometimes a woman but not often. One or two of the guys would be wearing leather or vinyl jackets, brown or black. There were always one or two stuffed pillows on the back window shelf that they apparently used to pass signals to each other. But what really made it easy to pick them out was that we would be driving down the highway (two or four lanes), we would vary our speed to try to notice other vehicles varying their speed with us. They knew what we were doing so often would not slow down. But as other traffic went by our vehicle, everyone always looked at us. We were in a G-Wagon with US flags on the plates, wearing US military uniforms. We were interesting. Everyone looked—except the Narcs.

The good ones made no bones about the fact that they were following us. They kept close and didn't care if we knew. They knew we could get away, and they made it harder by staying right on top of us. If there were a lot of vehicles involved, they would form a box around us, paralleling us on side roads, cars well in front and running drag behind us. With ten or twelve cars involved, it was still possible to break surveillance for a little while, but not for long.

Occasionally the Narcs had a good vehicle like a BMW or Volkswagon confiscated from a West German. They were faster than the G-Wagons and harder to notice because they blended in better. But the downside for the Narcs was that even they appreciated a fine automobile. If we wanted to blow off a Narc in a BMW, we just headed off road.

The good ones new we had an advantage at night and would not often waste their time pursuing us after dark. One afternoon I was with Steve Eairheart, and we were doing our best to cover a large Soviet column near Genthin. We were in an area that was a narrow gap with Permanent Restricted Areas bordering the road the column was using, leaving us only about a kilometer wide gap in which to work. The surveillance teams knew we would be there chasing the column, and even when they lost us it was only a matter of time until they found us again. As dark approached, we were on a main road, and, as we approached a railroad crossing, the traffic barrier came down. We had two car-loads of Narcs right behind us so we pulled up to the barrier as close as we could so that nothing could get in front of us and so that we could move forward as soon as the barrier lifted. As I watched the two surveillance team members in the vehicle right behind us (the BMW), the Narc in the passenger seat held up his left arm, pointed to his watch, and waived to us. It was exactly 6:00 p.m. They backed up, turned around, and left. No more surveillance for the rest of the night—at least from the Stasi.

• • •

Whatever the real reason, the surveillance was intense and persistent. As a result, blowing off surveillance became a part of the process I had to learn. There were lots of techniques, some subtle and some very blatant. I confess, there were times when not much was going on and blowing off surveillance became a kind of game. When there wasn't anything else to do, we practiced detecting and blowing the Narcs off. I found it particularly entertaining to find a way to lose them and then set somewhere and watch them try to find us.

If they were trying to be subtle, it sometimes worked to coast slowly to a stop at an intersection. They would creep up as slowly as they thought practical without being too obvious (surely they knew that we had made them) and, when it became obvious that we were just going to sit at the side of the road, stopped; they would coast around us, and, depending on the number of cars, one would go right, one left, and one straight ahead—slowly until they were out of sight. Of course, as soon as they were out of sight, we would turn around and make a high-speed run back down the road we had arrived on. If there wasn't a forth car waiting for us back down the road, this sometimes worked.

If they were being particularly blatant, we would find a point on the autobahn that was far from any exit with a steep bank off to the side and just stop the G-Wagon, make a sharp right turn off the autobahn straight down the hill. The G-Wagons were good four-wheel drive vehicles and could handle some pretty steep, rugged terrain. The Stasi would stop and just watch us as we drove across a field to another nearby road.

When it was serious and we needed to go in on a target within the next couple of hours, one of the most effective ways to get rid of the surveillance was to accelerate away from them, make a difficult but obvious turn to get off the road, but headed toward another installation in the area. They would assume that we were headed for the installation we turned toward and head directly there to set up around the installation that we were not going to. I confirmed this on several occasions because we would have a target list that included several installations in the area; feint toward one and go to another. After several hours we would wind up sneaking in on the installation that we had feinted toward earlier and encounter the Narcs around the installation. It was most satisfying when, due to superior knowledge of the target area resulting from thorough preparation with the target folders (and later due to lots of experience around Soviet and East German installations), we would manage to get in, accomplish our coverage of the installation, and encounter the Narcs surrounding the area on our way out. More than once I observed very startled looks on the faces of Stasi as we zipped past them smoking at their monitoring point.

One of the things that complicated the evasion process was the extensive system of Permanent Restricted Areas. The Soviets and East German security personnel knew that if we were in their area and needed to move from one area to another, we would respect the PRAs. The PRAs were large (around twenty percent of East Germany fell within PRA) and where they fell in close proximity along their boundaries, they formed natural choke points. If the Stasi lost us and there were a couple of PRA-based choke points in the area, they would go there and wait for us to pass through to try to pick us up again.

I also learned that there were times that you didn't want to blow the security. If you lost them and they were serious, they could take inordinate measures to find you and get on you again. In that situation, you could lose them and often had a couple of hours to cover some targets before being picked up again. If they made the effort to find you again, they were likely to be extremely persistent and not very subtle the second time. So it was best to keep in mind the distance from the target and the amount of time you might need so as not to blow them off too early. It was also enjoyable to make a sudden break when the surveillance team had been lulled into a sense that you didn't know they were there.

Because of our capability with night-vision devices of which the Stasi did not seem to have any, the best technique was to lose the surveillance in the dark, move all night to the vicinity of key targets moving on back roads and trails to get close, and then hit the targets early in the morning before the surveillance got organized and out in force. That explained a lot of our night departures and why we didn't get much sleep at night.

• • •

One night, by coincidence, here were four tour teams at the Potsdam House. Two teams were returning from tours (one air team, one ground team) and one team on the Local. Todd Milton and one of the NCOs pulled into the house around 1900 and came in complaining that the surveillance was so thick on them that they couldn't get started on their tour. The surveillance was so persistent that they were simply riding his bumper and the team had not been able to shake them, so they had returned to the Potsdam House. We all got up, went out, and manned all four G-Wagons and raced out the front gate and down the entry road to Route 2. Then we all began to peel off in different directions. The surveillance team picked the wrong car to follow and Todd got off on his mission. The rest of us returned to the Potsdam House and had dinner. It was just part of the game.

Chapter 6

Style

Everyone had a slightly different approach to touring. During the first few tours when I was back seating with other tour officers, I watched how they prepared for a tour, how they conducted it, how they reported.; how they interacted with the NCO drivers, how they dealt with surveillance, how aggressive they were in various circumstances and against various types of targets. Once I started touring on my own, I got a lot of advice from the NCOs. New tour officers did not automatically warrant respect from the NCOs, and the NCOs were pretty free with their advice. They were all tight-lipped about the specifics of how other officers conducted themselves (what happened on the road, stayed on the road). But they didn't mind telling you how they thought something should be done, how aggressive we should be. I listened. I figured the NCOs' skin was on the line just like mine, and they had a right to be in on decisions that could get us in trouble. Just like the officers, some NCOs were extremely aggressive, some were more cautious. This was all relative; everyone, officers and NCOs alike, were pretty aggressive. You had to be or you came back with nothing from your tour. You couldn't collect good intelligence cruising the autobahns kilometers from the installations and training areas.

The NCOs were a spur. They never said anything directly, but you didn't want to be a wimp in their eyes. They saw all of the tour officers in action and had their favorites. In most cases, they liked the combination of aggressiveness and common sense. Tours were often hours of driving around

East Germany without seeing much. When you finally discovered some military activity worth covering, adrenalin levels went up and the excitement began. The tour finally became interesting. As a tour officer, the NCOs expected you to be aggressive.

As my first year progressed I developed my own touring "style." I became familiar with most of the primary installations and training areas—Soviet and East German. I got familiar with navigating my way through the various Permanent Restricted Areas, choke points, back roads, and trails that were necessary to approach any target without being detected. I learned how to set up my equipment so that I could get at all of it quickly in any situation—night or day. I had five Nikon F-3 cameras with titanium bodies and power winders equipped with a range of lenses that I kept within reach. I carried lenses ranging from 28mm wide angles to 1000mm telephotos with doublers that could extend even that. I taught myself the best film settings to use for any lens and any situation. I kept a Canon Sureshot 35mm lens handily available so that if I got out of the G-Wagon I could carry it in my pocket, out of sight. I taped a Lanier cassette recorder to the dashboard, where both the NCO and I could reach it to turn it on. I carried dozens of spare batteries and at least fifty rolls of 35mm film (mostly black and white but a few rolls of color). I learned how to pack maps so that they were easy to get at.

I carried "tools." I carried a pry bar in case we needed to break a lock (didn't happen often but I used it from time to time). I carried a small garden hand rake for digging through Soviet campfires to rescue bits and pieces of papers left behind after exercises (used regularly). I carried flashlights with both white and red lenses. Night vision was important. As an infantry officer, I had learned to read maps in the dark by the light of a red filtered flashlight. I did it a hundred times more often as a USMLM tour officer.

Night vision goggles were kept in a separate bag but with the onset of nightfall were moved to an easily accessible place along with my 500,000-candle-power spotlight and my handheld infrared spotlight. I had inherited the infrared spotlight from a departing tour officer, and I don't think I ever went on a tour that I did not use it at least once.

I taught myself to memorize routes into and out of installations and training areas so I didn't have to look at maps when things got hot. One of the most productive things I did during my first year (I never stopped doing it) was to spend every minute that something wasn't going on to familiarize myself with ways into and out of Soviet installations and training areas. When they were empty, I spent hours driving around in training areas. At some later time when we encountered activity in the training area or at an installation, I usually knew the routes in and around the facility better than those reacting to our presence. The NCOs were a fount of knowledge about routes. They spent about thirty percent more time on the road than the officers, and they visited the various installations even more frequently. So, if we started into a recon on an installation and training area, I always asked the NCOs what they thought the best way in was or if they knew of other routes. They always did, and I would have them show me.

I developed my own style of aggressiveness. My preference was to sneak in on an installation or activity, photograph everything, and sneak away without being seen if I could. I will say that it didn't work that often, and usually at some point we would be seen and the local garrison or unit would react in some way. But by being sneaky, I think I got a lot more information before we had to run for it if I had been aggressive from the beginning. Sometimes to get the final piece of important information, you had to get close enough to be seen. In that case, you just got in as close as you could, camera ready, got your shots, and ran for it. It worked pretty well, but there wasn't much hanging around to gather more. And sometimes, the "Paul Nelson-run-through-the-middle" was the only way. Best conducted as a total surprise to the target and with a clean, unobstructed get-away route planned—preferably to a nearby paved road where we usually had the speed advantage. I learned and practiced all the techniques. Sometimes you had to provoke them intentionally to get your information. I remember one time with LTC Mike Peters, our new Chief of Ground, back-seating with me on one of his new-guy training tours; we were checking out a unit on a ridge line and had gotten about as much info as we could by sneaking around. But we still did not have any clues as to who they were. In order to get a vehicle registration number to identify the unit, I had the driver, SGT Steve Eairhardt, expose our vehicle to the unit we were working against and simply waited until they sent a vehicle to chase us away. I made Mike Peters pretty nervous, as he was in the backseat looking directly out the window at the approaching vehicle until the very last second when I could read the vehicle registration number. As I got the vehicle registration number I yelled for Steve to run and we began to accelerate away. The approaching Soviet vehicle closed to within thirty or forty meters of us before we began to rapidly accelerate away. They chased us for a couple miles but finally gave up. And we had a clue to the identity of unit with the vehicle registration number. Sometimes you just had to provoke them to get what you needed.

I learned to read soldiers, particularly guards. I always thought I was pretty good at reading people. Guards came in all types. Sometimes they were serious and attentive. Sometimes they were lax and indifferent. The East German soldiers were more dangerous (in my opinion) than the Soviet soldiers. They were more likely to take their guard-duty responsibilities seriously and react. They were less likely to fire a shot, but they were more likely to alert their superiors and send someone out to chase you off. An important lesson that I learned early was that the East Germans had second rate equipment compared to the Sovs. So taking big risks around an East German unit or garrison didn't make much sense.

But reading Soviet soldiers was an art. They were all conscripts, which meant none of them were particularly enthusiastic. They were more likely to be attentive and to react if there was an officer nearby. No officer: they might not react at all.

The first threshold was seeing if they had weapons. If there were no weapons then no matter what we were pretty safe in the short run. However, the second part of that equation was that the Sovs did not have the same degree of weapons and ammunition discipline present in US units. Every time a US soldier was issued a weapon in a peacetime environment it was tightly controlled. The only time he was likely to have ammunition was if he was on guard duty. And then the rounds would be few and counted carefully at the end of the guard duty to ensure that every round issued was accounted for. Not so with Soviet soldiers. Their weapon might be lying off in the grass. On a lonely guard post, the soldier might have a couple of boxes of ammunition, set up some tin cans, and have some target practice. We saw plenty of evidence of this.

But I learned to read the signs. The first thing I learned to accept was that, no matter how lax I thought a soldier was, someone had assigned to him a special zone in which he was supposed to protect "something." Some soldiers took this seriously, and some did not. But at some point all of them thought that they might get in trouble if they didn't do something if you pushed too hard into their zone of responsibility. So I watched for signals. Soldiers on foot without weapons or radios were generally ignored unless they acted very agitated. Or if they really seemed bored I might stop and talk to them. I carried a heavy load of small sandwiches and a couple of cartons of cigarettes which I passed out liberally. It was surprising what a bored solder supplied with a couple of sandwiches and a pack of Marlboros would tell you. Soldiers with weapons that saw us but did not appear to react could be by-passed or sometimes even talked to if they seemed non-reactive. But if a soldier saw us, watched us attentively, or touched his weapon it was time to go. No further provocation.

The problem or danger, if you will, was that it was pretty hard to know what the soldier's zone of responsibility might be or what he was tasked to guard. The way I saw it, if a soldier saw us, he only had a couple of options. He could ignore us. They sometimes did. He could watch us closely, and if we were not in his zone of responsibility and we bypassed him he would continue to do nothing. But if he decided he needed to react and began sending signals (calling to others, touching his rifle), he was sending us a big signal. "You are in my zone of responsibility, and I want you to leave." If you left, that resolved the issue for most Soviet guards. You were out of his zone of responsibility. If he took this step and you didn't leave, what was his next step? Unshoulder his weapon and act as if he might shoot. If you were dumb enough not to leave at that point, I figured you should simply come home with a car full of bullet holes. Of course, if all other signals were ignored, the soldier's last resort was to fire. This seemed to happen frequently enough to tour teams that it was clear that the Soviets had not given their soldiers any instructions that would stop them from firing.

In my mind, the absolute greatest danger that a tour team faced was a situation in which you entered a Soviet guard's area of responsibility, the guard went through a series of what could be considered warning signals (pay close attention, wave or call out in a hostile manner, unshoulder his weapon), but no one on the team saw the soldier or the signals. A soldier caught by surprise (goofing off in the wrong spot, taking a nap, whatever) and surprised by the presence of a Mission vehicle might run through the entire sequence pretty quickly and before the tour team even saw him. Seeing the guards, knowing when and where they should normally be or how they normally were positioned, became important. I thought that one of the factors that contributed to shootings was the lack of accountability for ammunition. If a guard popped off a couple of rounds at you, he didn't have to report it to anyone.

It was a little later, during my second year and I was with SSG John Johnson running a ridge near Ohrdruf Training area in southwest East Germany. We were checking out a small bivouac site that I had checked a dozen times before without ever seeing any evidence of use. I was sure we weren't going to see anything this time, and I was glancing through Time Magazine as we were driving down the trail. Suddenly, Johnny said, "There's a tank."

I said (somewhat incredulously), "Where?"

He said, "Right *there*," pointing twenty meters away.

Sure enough, there was a T-62 tank parked behind a couple of trees just off the trail. Down went my hands for my Nikon 'Grab Camera' that I kept on the floor of the G-Wagon, and I came up firing away. I yelled for John to get us out of there. This all happened so fast that I didn't realize until I got my photos back a couple of days later that there was a Soviet Lieutenant in front of the tank with a ferocious look on his face waving his fists at us.

John tore off down the road about two hundred meters where there was a trail leading off to the left. I yelled for him to turn left on the trail, thinking that we would get behind the tanks (I was sure there was more than one) and see if we could get a better look.

As we turned left and started down the trail about fifty meters, a tree came crashing down across the road from the right blocking further progress. From behind a couple of small pines on the right, a Soviet soldier with an AK-47 stepped out. He leveled the AK at our windshield.

I looked at him and saw the hint of a grin. He knew he had caught us by surprise. I said to John, "Back up. He's not going to shoot."

John said, "Are you sure?"

I said, "Yeah, back up." And then I leaned out the window and gave the soldier a big grin and a wave. The soldier dropped his rifle to his side and returned my grin as we backed up. We turned and made a run back from the direction we came.

I'm not sure exactly how I knew the soldier wasn't going to shoot. I had just learned how to gauge reactions, and while the rifle was pointed he just didn't look like he was very upset. But it was part of what you had to learn.

• • •

Some tour officers and NCOs seemed not to need sleep. I wasn't one of them. If there was a lot of adrenalin flowing, I could go for hours. But if it was a normal tour I could run for about twenty or so hours and then I needed to get a couple of hours sleep. I watched the NCOs. With the exception of SSG Randy Everett, whom I don't think ever slept a wink on tour, I thought most of them were a lot like me. They needed periodic breaks. So I developed a style for getting some rest.

My favorite solution was to find a highly-trafficked rail line and find a secluded spot where we could hear trains coming in the distance and watch them pass. The best spots were where we could see the train pass under lights of some kind—particularly if the light was bright enough for pictures. The next best solution was a sleeping spot that facilitated chasing the train to a lighted spot for pictures. I guess enough of the other tour officers followed this same procedure that one of the mission jokes was waking up as you hear a train go by and to see a string of chemical transport rail cars passing, which to sleepy eyes often appeared to be Soviet BTR-60 Armored Personnel Carriers. We called them "Midnight BTRs."

Another resting spot (particularly during the Great T-80 Hunt—more on that later) was to park right in the middle of a military tactical trail (Tac Trail) that tanks, armored personnel carriers, and self-propelled artillery were known to use. My thinking was that if a tank column came along they would stop and tell you to get out of the way—I doubted if they would really run us over. Normally, I wanted to be somewhere that, even while resting, you had the chance of picking something up.

There were some occasions that we were really tired and just needed a safe place to sleep for two or three hours. In every region of East Germany over the first year, I found small hideouts high on a ridge or buried in a heavy wood line. Even that wasn't always so safe. I woke up after a couple of hours sleep one morning with a German Forest Meister pounding on the hood of the G-Wagon. He was irritated that we were in his forest. But sleeping more than a couple of hours at a time was rare.

• • •

"Risk versus Gain." It was the unofficial Mission motto. You were constantly expected to evaluate the risks you were taking against the potential intelligence gain. The official Mission position (which I agreed with fully) was that there was no intelligence gain that was going to be obtained by a tour team that was worth getting killed for. But to know what was a good "gain," you had to understand what was valuable. It took me about a year to start really understanding this point. The key was listening to briefings and the comments of the Mission production officer. The production officer was the one who read through all of our Mission "highlights" and ran through our pictures to see if we had hit on something really worth reporting. He had a list of intelligence collection requirements that were prioritized by importance. The production officer worked with the ground operations officer to plan tour targets. As a tour officer when you received your list of targets for an upcoming mission, it would include specific activities to be accomplished at that site. Most of it was pretty straightforward, like "check the activity at a local garrison," or "acquire vehicle registration numbers for vehicles inside a garrison," or "check for the presence of a certain type of vehicle." We were constantly looking for evidence of changes to Soviet or East German force structure and upgrades to equipment types.

To prepare for a tour you needed to check with the production officer to get a real sense of what important collection targets were likely or possible at targets on our route. But there were always some general "big" intelligence objectives that were on the hot list. Almost the entire time that I was at the Mission we were gathering evidence of the introduction of the SS-20 missile into East Germany. It was an intermediate range missile that, deployed into East Germany, gave the Soviets the opportunity to strike at NATO facilities anywhere in Europe with virtually no notice. *That* was important.

The fact was, though, to gather *any* intelligence you had to take risks. You had to get close to garrisons, you had to get close to units in training areas. If you were going to generate any reports of value, if you were going to make a contribution, you had to get close.

For me, I figured that you had to be good enough at what you were doing that you could get close without incurring too much risk. There was no such thing as a risk-free tour.

I learned other risk-related lessons. For operational security reasons, the Soviets established a series of UPS all across East Germany. In the event of a real conflict with the West, this established a bunch of "plug-in" points for communications as units moved forward toward the inter-German border.

Rather than relying exclusively on vulnerable radio transmissions as units moved forward, they had plug-in points for wired communications. It was a good approach to communications security. We knew about the system and had plotted a number of them. The system was an underground system but had access points identified by small, two-meter by two-meter sheds in various locations scattered across East Germany.

I was tasked to do a survey of known UPS points. We had identified about forty such sites throughout East Germany. On a day in which our coverage was shifting from Area B to Area C, I was tasked to cover about seventy-five percent of them over forty-eight hours. I plotted a route, started in the north, and worked my way south. It was an elaborate system with several different components. I was confirming exact locations and components included in each UPS point. Inside of each surface shed was a ground-level hatch leading to a small underground component room. None of the points were locked, although all were latched. The equipment was all in good shape and well-maintained. Some UPS were alarmed with pressure detent pins in the hatches. Most were in remote locations, a few on the edge of towns.

Smitty was my driver, and we worked our way south getting details in each location. Sometimes we finished the coverage and backed off in the woods to watch to see if anyone would react to the alarms. I was sensitive to the fact that we were setting a definite pattern running north to south, potentially setting off alarms that if centrally monitored anywhere could be setting us up for an ambush somewhere in the south. We became cautious as we approached each UPS trying to detect any evidence of a setup.

I don't think that there was a central monitoring point, but late on the second day we encountered a UPS that was different. It was on the edge of a town and surrounded by two layers of concertina wire and barbed-wire gates. It took me several minutes to untangle the wire, securing the barbed-wire gates, and then to get down into the UPS control room. As I went down I saw the alarm detent. I gathered the data and was exiting when I heard Smitty rev the G-Wagon engine, which was the signal that he saw someone coming. It was already dark, so I knew they had to be close. I wanted to leave the UPS as we found it, so I quickly rewired the barbed-wire gates as best I could and ran for the car. As I jumped in Smitty began backing away from the UPS.

"There's a motorcycle coming down the road right toward us," Smitty whispered.

I could see the headlight coming fast. We backed farther into the shadows and watched as a Volkespolizei officer road up on his motorcycle, jumped off, and went over to check the UPS. He checked the two outer gates but did not go into the shed. I guess that he was satisfied that it was an accidental alarm. We waited for him to leave and then drifted on to the next site.

I learned two lessons from this episode that I added to my methods. First, look for alarms and don't underestimate them. Second, putting things back the way you found them was worth the effort.

Chapter 7
Reporting

I mentioned earlier I was very competitive. I've always tried to be the best at whatever I was assigned, and the Mission was no exception. I wanted to be a good tour officer, if not the best. As my training progressed, I began watching other tour officers to see how they were doing. Some officers were respected for their aggressiveness and field touring techniques—but I noticed that was mostly among tour officers and tour NCOs. Of course, I wanted the respect of my peers so I listened to those things which seemed to carry the most weight with them. But that counted for nothing when it came to our annual personnel evaluations. What I was interested in was what most impressed the senior leadership of the mission—meaning for me, the Chief of the Ground Section (initially LTC Greg Govan; later LTC Mike Peters and MAJ John Eschrich) and the Chief of Mission (COL Randy Greenwalt followed by COL Roland Lajoie and COL Bill Haloran). I noticed that they had several "favorites" among the tour officers. Initially I thought it might be because these tour officers were the most aggressive or the most successful at penetrating targets. Of course, these factors were elements of what led to the evaluation of high performance because without them you could not return from a tour or mission with any information of value. But what really made the favorites stand out was reporting. A tour officer could have the most exciting tour that ever occurred and might observe the sexiest, most high-tech equipment that the Soviets ever deployed into East Germany. Or a tour officer might acquire incredibly good close-up handheld photography of Soviet military activity. But if these activities were not properly documented, they never counted for anything more than a good war story. To get real credit and become of value, the information had to be reported through the mission system, ultimately coming out the far end as an "intelligence report" or IIR. As an infantry officer, my experience with intelligence was really as a consumer of low-level tactical intelligence—not as a producer of intelligence. So I had a steep learning curve in front of me.

Like everything else at the mission, there was no formal training program for report writing—you just picked it up as you went along.

I noticed that, of my contemporaries, Clyde Evans seemed to have achieved some degree of recognition with the Mission leadership. I had known Clyde for about four years (Naval Postgraduate School (NPS), Defense Language Institute (DLI) in Monterey, and the US Army Russian Institute (USARI)) as a reasonable student, half-way decent skier, and the class prankster. But I did not recollect any particular recognition achieved by Clyde while we were attending the NPS, DLI, or USARI. I knew that he didn't miss deadlines, but I had never heard anyone say anything special about his writing. But he seemed to have caught the attention of LTC Govan and COL Greenwalt. Clyde and I were pretty good friends already, so, ever mindful of his practical jokes, I began spending time with him to see if I could figure out what he was doing that made him special. Almost immediately it became apparent that the area in which he excelled was his disciplined approach to report writing. I will claim nothing original in my comments that follow. Clyde had a good approach and I copied it.

The mission published lots of reports, but from the tour officer's perspective there were four key reports due at the conclusion of every mission into East Germany.

The first two were directly related: a highlight report, completed immediately on return from a tour, and which quickly summarized the most important events of the tour; followed by a more detailed mission report that listed virtually everything seen by the tour team while deployed on a mission, including all photography. The third type of report was based on the mission report; the tour officer might be tasked to produce one or more formal intelligence reports (IIR) providing detailed information about a single item from the tour report. Finally, every target folder for the targets that the team covered had to be updated to ensure that the next team deploying to this target would have the latest information about the site.

The three allied missions (USMLM, BRIXMIS and FMLM) were physically located in the various sectors of West Berlin. Liaison teams from all of the Missions deployed initially into East Germany across the Glienecke Bridge in the southwest corner of West Berlin. This bridge was manned only by Soviet guards and not East German Border Guards. It was used almost exclusively by the Missions, although some may remember that this was also the bridge on which Gary Powers, the U-2 pilot, shot down over the Soviet Union in the '60s was exchanged for a Soviet spy in 1962.

There is a point to this digression. All allied mission liaison teams returning from East Germany completed a highlight report *immediately* on their return. The reason why will become clear in a couple of minutes. But because the US Military Liaison Mission headquarters in West Berlin was closest of the three to the Glienecke Bridge, the first stop for *all* liaison teams from all of the missions into East Germany was at USMLM, where they completed the mission highlight report before continuing on to their own mission or home for a shower or to get some rest. Regardless of time of day, regardless of how tired or hungry they were, this was the first action of every liaison team on return from a mission into East Germany.

The mission highlight report was intended to give a "down and dirty" summary of what the liaison team had observed during its tour. The first paragraph was a quick overview, would detail the areas visited, and might say something like "quiet tour not much to report," or "major rail movement observed at Gross Ammensleben," or "significant drivers training activity near Halle." If a serious incident had occurred it would be highlighted here also. For example, it could contain entries such as "team detained for six hours in Koenigsbruek training area" and would include enough detail from each activity observed that those reviewing the report could gather a sense of what was going on and what Soviet and East German units were active in the area that the team toured. If an incident has occurred, sufficient detail was provided to allow following teams deploying to the same area to avoid the point at which the incident occurred or at least take special precautions if they returned to the same area. When completed, a copy of the report was placed in a box for each mission and either picked up by returning liaison teams or delivered to the other missions each morning.

Who read these highlight reports? First and foremost, they were read by other liaison teams deploying into East Germany. My last stop before every trip into East Germany was to check the latest highlight to get a sense of what was going on. In USMLM the highlights were reviewed every morning by the chief of the ground section (for Army teams) and the intel production officer who looked for items that needed to be reported immediately or to which a departing liaison team might need to be re-directed.

From the perspective of the tour officer writing the report (okay, from my perspective), the highlight report was a "love-hate" relationship. If I had an exciting tour (lots going on, lots to report) and my driver and I returned at 0200 it might mean that I would be working on the mission highlight until 0400 or even 0500. On the other hand, for a boring tour the mission highlight might only take fifteen or twenty minutes. But a mission highlight was turned in for every trip into East Germany—even for what we called "Culturals." More on that later.

I studied Clyde's highlights. He was Mr. Efficient. No wasted words; precise and to the point. When you finished reading Clyde's mission highlight, you knew where he had been, what he had seen, what he thought was important, and whether or not anything had happened that other teams should watch out for. To keep the quality of the reporting up, the Chief of the Ground Section, Greg Govan, graded the highlights submitted by all ground teams. I had to settle for the best grade of B+ along with the comment "work on your handwriting." My handwriting only got worse.

In perspective, the highlight was the easiest part of the reporting process. It was mandatory and had to be completed before you could go home. You could write a poor report but you couldn't get behind. The most difficult part of the reporting process for most liaison officers (at least as I observed during my four years at the mission) was the detailed mission report. This report was used to capture every detail of intelligence worthy information that a team observed while on tour. Most teams used small handheld tape recorders to capture verbal descriptions of activities observed in real time. I had a small Lanier micro-recorder that I taped to the Gelandewagon dashboard, placed where the record button could be reached by either myself, in the passenger seat, or by the driver. On encountering anything of interest, the first thing that we did was turn on the tape recorder and begin describing the activity. A good tour— one with a lot of activity by the Soviets and East Germans—might result in two or three tapes completely full of verbal descriptions. In many cases, both the driver and the officer would be talking simultaneously, reporting different types of information. Detailed de-taping could be a tedious process.

This was even more complicated. Normally a tour officer was "on pass," meaning that he was accredited to the headquarters, GSFG, for about six weeks at a time; he had a "pass" or documentation to get into East Germany (kind of like a "get into jail" card). During that time the tour officer would probably spend three to four twenty-four-hour periods actually in East Germany each week; the remainder of the week back in West Berlin. Once the mission highlight report was completed (before going home at the end of a tour), the majority of the time between tours was spent preparing for the next tour. For most liaison officers, detailed mission reports were completed during the six week period when you were "off-pass" and not traveling on intelligence gathering missions.

But Clyde was efficient. He carefully stored all materials obtained on a given tour—notes, tapes, photography, physical materials gathered one way or another during the tour—in a way that kept it organized and ready for him as soon as he was ready to work on it. After six weeks of touring, getting little sleep, and taking possibly hundreds of photographs, it was often quite difficult to remember clearly events that occurred during the first couple of weeks. But here again, I found one of Clyde's efficiencies. He was *very* disciplined with his on-pass time. He got his highlights in on time, and he did thorough preparations for his next tour. Where he was unique was that he spent every spare minute that he was not prepping for his next mission working on the mission reports. Often he would manage to finish or nearly finish his mission reports before the end of his on-pass period. Watching him, I carried away a commitment to get my mission reports done while I was still on pass. I think that once I got in the rhythm I was fairly efficient also. The best part about this efficiency was that it left the tour officer (Clyde and me) with a lot of free time during the off-pass period to work on other things—which paid off in the long run.

I don't know if this was always the case at the Mission but the entire time that I was there we always had at least one full-time intelligence officer to fill a position called the "production officer". The production officer was responsible for being aware of existing intelligence requirements—particularly those which might be subject to the reconnaissance activities of our liaison teams and proposing such targets of opportunity to the ground operations officer (who was scheduling and designating targets for tours). The production officer also reviewed highlight and mission reports to identify items that should be formally reported by the Mission to the rest of the intelligence world. He often wrote or produced intelligence reports himself based on the mission reports. But, as frequently, he would find elements in a mission report that needed to be reported but that could only be properly done by the tour officer that actually observed the activity and would task that officer to write the report (in my experience, he would badger that officer unmercifully until the report was done). The production officer was one of our qualified (and usually most experienced) tour officers. But the importance of the production officer's responsibilities was such that he could not be away often, so he toured only about one-third of the time that other tour officers. I was happy that the position was reserved for intel officers. As I recall, all of the production officers that I knew all would have preferred the tour officer position. So the process was that tour officers executed their missions and described what they observed in the mission highlight report and the thorough mission report. The production officer, and often the chief of ground identified intelligence-report worthy observations and directed the tour officers to write them.

An example of how the Mission reporting system worked comes to mind as I write this. I was my second year of being a tour officer, and I considered myself pretty experienced by then and quite aggressive. Early one morning we were working the local area and found a train loaded with T-64 tanks setting on a seldom used rail siding. It was early morning—first light—and the tank crews were buttoned up tight inside the tanks and were just beginning to pop the hatches to get some fresh air. There was a light snow on the ground, and a light dusting of snow on the tanks. Honestly, to my infantry eyes, it was a pretty sight. So I told my driver, SGT Steve Eairhardt, to just run down alongside of the tanks. We would make one pass; he would get the vehicle markings and I would take pictures. The whole train was T-64s, nothing new or spectacular (or so I thought), so I just decided to get some real close-ups using my 500mm lens on tanks that were about thirty to fifty meters away. It was uneventful. We ran the siding. I shot up a roll of film and cleared the area. The rest of the tour was pretty slow. At the end of the tour we returned to Berlin and I submitted my highlight report along with my photos for developing. I went home and crashed. When I arrived the next morning I was met by the Chief of Ground (LTC Mike Peters) with a handful of my photos and a task to get to work right away on an intelligence report. What the production officer had picked up in my pictures that I didn't even notice was that I had gotten very detailed, close-up photography of a new type of bolt-on armor that potentially gave Soviet tanks greater protection from current US anti-tank weapons.

I am not going to say too much about the intelligence reports. These reports are what established the Mission as a premier intelligence-gathering source. We had direct access to the largest and most powerful forces of the primary threat to the United States. We were trained, experienced observers and totally reliable (in comparison to other HUMINT sources). We were well connected with the entire US Intelligence Community, and we maintained our status by checking our own data and providing details that were not available from other sources. And if there was a single measurable factor that affected a tour officer's efficiency report it was the number of IIRs produced each year. The number of IIRs a tour officer might generate during a year was based on time on the road and "luck."

When I first joined the Army, one of my instructors in Army ROTC had defined "luck" as "preparation meeting opportunity." Never was that truer than during my time as a tour officer. Time spent preparing for a mission meant that you were usually prepared to take advantage of opportunities encountered along the way. A light-hearted example comes to mind.

During my second year at the Mission we got a new Chief of Mission— Colonel Roland LaJoie. He was a squared-away guy, and I had the pleasure of working for him three times in my Army career. As he familiarized himself with his responsibilities at USMLM he was aware that tour officers were quite aggressive and he determined to observe us all in action so that he would have a sense of what we were doing and what conditions that we operated under in East Germany. So, during his first couple of months at the mission he went on tours as a third man in the vehicle with each of the tour officers—a practice that he continued on a periodic basis throughout his time at USMLM. When it came to be my turn with the colonel in my back seat, I knew that first impressions were everything—even at the Mission. So I spent extra time on my preparations for the tour on which he would be present.

One of the targets on my target list was a small training area on the north side of the East German city, Wittenberg, known to host training exercises for a nearby SCUD Missile battalion. I had been to this site a number of times and never seen anything at all in the training area—but I studied the target folders again for likely dispositions of equipment and reviewed SCUD photos to be sure that I was as ready as I could be.

This target training area was on the south end of what we called the local area, and tours for the local always started at 1500; so around 1330 my driver, SSG Jesse Schatz, and I gathered up the colonel and crossed the Glienicke Bridge into East Germany and headed south on Route 2, just to get a feel for what was going on. It was late summer/early fall but a clear day with no overcast. As we approached the southern end of the local area, I took us to the southern edge of the training area that I thought would give us better access before being discovered. As we approached the main bivouac site I thought I saw something through the trees and told Jesse to stop about three hundred or four hundred meters away. A quick survey with my binoculars confirmed in my mind that the SCUDs were present. They were difficult to see through the trees, but I could clearly see a distinctive door on the side of the vehicle that confirmed they were SCUDs. It didn't hurt knowing that they often deployed to this site, so I was actually looking for them. Colonel Lajoie couldn't believe it. He spent some time with the binoculars but couldn't pick them out. They looked like they were in an admin break and not actively engaged in training, so I figured that we could get closer safely. I told Jesse to follow the trail that led to the bivouac site and to just drive right on past them. We wound up driving beside three launchers at a range of about fifty feet. Colonel Lajoie was appropriately impressed. I was lucky. It was the first time that I had ever seen SCUDs up close myself, and the first time I had ever seen any unit deployed in the Wittenberg training area. But I was prepared and took advantage of the situation. Luck: when opportunity meets preparation. I say lucky because it gave me the opportunity to get off on a good foot with the new chief of mission.

My real point here is that the opportunity to submit intelligence reports was always based partly on luck. As a tour officer you could not set out to create a sighting or situation that would result in a need to write an IIR. But if you prepared yourself in advance, when opportunities presented themselves you were ready to take advantage of them. As a tour officer you could work your butt off trying to capture information worth the submission of an IR but encountering an opportunity to exercise your preparations was not always in your hands. Another example: I remember that during the year that the Soviets introduced the

T-80 tank into East Germany, Nick Nicholson—one of our smartest tour officers made a concerted effort to be the first to obtain handheld photography of the new tank—he studied the information that we had gathered to date and decided that the Koenigsbruek training area just north of Dresden was the place most likely to produce results. Then he took information on the training area that was in the target folders (I had been documenting routes in and out of the training area for several months). He plotted a route into the training area and selected a place from which to observe that he thought a team could remain undiscovered for several days. Then he and his driver, SSG Jim McDowall, slipped into the training area under cover of darkness and stayed for nearly a full week trying to get that illusive first handheld photograph of the T-80 tank. He had done all that could be done to prepare himself to get that photo. But that second part of luck—opportunity—was not with him. The tanks never passed the part of the training area that he and Jim could observe.

The final part of the reporting process was easy to overlook and never get around to and that was updating target folders. It was a tedious task—all done by hand using drawings and maps and adding photos where useful. But it took time, and no one ever checked to see if you had done it. But it was probably the most significant data necessary to the next team that would visit the site. Some tour officers did a great job, some not so great. Important targets could have folders that had a couple hundred pages of details spanning a number of years. On the other end of the scale, the target folder might be for a new target and only have a page or two of information. Often, tours were tasked to investigate such a target and to complete the target folder. Once identified, targets rarely got dropped from the mission database. A completed target folder usually included:

- 1:50,000 scale map showing the outline of the target and annotated to indicate ingress and egress routes
- A descriptive page explaining what a tour might expect to see at that location
- Photos of deployments, activities, and equipment previously observed at the site
- Annotation of maps and descriptions of where security measures were encountered and reactions by local units to the presence of a USMLM team

- Other details that seemed relevant or appropriate

So, this was both the heart and the tedium of being a tour officer at USMLM. As exciting as the job could be on the road, the work was not over until the paperwork was done. And like every other job I had in the Army (or anyplace else for that matter), paperwork was tedious. No one ever stands around the water cooler talking about the great highlight or mission report that he had just written. But to do it right, it had to be done. Clyde Evans had a good system. I copied it and it worked for me.

As a tour officer I was frequently informed by others that the IIRs produced at USMLM were greatly valued in the Intelligence Community, but I never fully understood this until I moved on to my next assignment, which was as the Chief of the Warsaw Pact Ground Forces Order of Battle Section in the Defense Intelligence Agency. There, I had thirty-five analysts that tracked every last tank and truck owned by the forces of the Warsaw Pact. The analysts poured over USMLM ground team reports for clues and insights into the structure of the Warsaw Pact ground forces. USMLM reporting was reliable, detailed, and consistent. Follow-up taskings could be levied. Clarifications could be obtained. Used in conjunction with other sources, USMLM reporting was the Rosetta Stone that provided the key to understanding many intelligence issues.

Chapter 8
A Rookie No More

Somewhere around the end of my rookie year and the first part of my second year I began to feel confident in my role as a USMLM tour officer. I had been running the ground team's vehicle-recognition training and seen enough on the road that I felt I knew the vehicle ID. I had been to virtually all of the major and hundreds of minor sites throughout East Germany. For the main targets I had been there enough to know the best, most secretive routes in and out. I had gotten good at spotting surveillance and blowing them off. I knew how to plan and prepare a mission. I knew my equipment and how to use it. I had had a few close calls and had come out of them unscathed. I was on top of my reporting. I knew the NCO drivers—knew what to expect from them in various situations and had gained credibility with them in my capabilities. I was ready. There was no sacred ceremony, I simply declared to myself that I was no longer a rookie, and I was ready to be a full-fledged tour officer.

As it turns out, I was ready for the closest call that I had during my four years as a liaison officer at USMLM. And as ready as I thought I was, I made a rookie mistake.

My task was simple. The Russians had two radio intercept battalions in East Germany just packed full of sexy equipment. We didn't see them often and when we did we tried to get good photography. One of the battalions was in the north and routinely deployed along the northern part of the East/West German border when a large NATO exercise was scheduled for northern West

Germany (British sector). Likewise, the southern battalion deployed along the southern East German border when a major NATO exercise was scheduled for the US Sector in West Germany. As luck would have it, a large exercise was coming up in the north, and I was tasked to check a couple of bivouac sites the northern battalion had been known to use before.

My driver for the trip was SGT Charles Smith (Smitty). Smitty was new and was still in his training phase, so SSG Mike Poindexter would be back-seating with us and keeping an eye on Smitty's driving. I scheduled our departure from Potsdam so that we would hit the first site right at first light with minimum risk of reaction by the troops and good light for photography. Everything went perfectly. We arrived at the first bivouac site and the intercept unit was there. Not only were they present, they had all of their equipment deployed for easy photographic coverage. The unit was deployed along the edge of a wood line facing a newly plowed farmer's field. The wood line jutted into the plowed field like a small peninsula, and equipment, vehicles, antennas, and small Soviet ten-man tents could be seen all along the edge of the field. It looked like everyone was still in their tents, asleep. There wasn't even anyone outside taking an early morning leak. We could see everything. I had my titanium-bodied Nikon F3 with 500mm lens ready to go on "rock and roll." We started into the plowed field circling the camp at about fifty meters from the wood line. The light was perfect, and I was sure that I was getting good pictures.

Suddenly I felt the G-wagon begin to bog down slightly, and Smitty let the vehicle lose momentum. I felt it settle into the soft soil of the plowed field and come to a stop. Mike Poindexter began shouting instructions to Smitty. I was sure that we could rock the vehicle free, but we were making a lot of noise. We began to wake up the Sov encampment. I could feel that with each forward and backward rocking motion the vehicle was getting ready to break loose and get going, but more and more soldiers emerged from the tent city to see what was going on. I would guess that by the time the vehicle was steadily moving again we had an audience of about fifty soldiers and officers. We made a beeline across the field to the nearest paved road and departed at high speed without further incident.

Now, you ask, where was the danger in that episode? Well, that is not the end of the story. I decided that this equipment was so sexy and of such great interest to the US Intel Community that we could let things cool down for about four hours and then make another run at the deployment from across the plowed field. My reasoning was that they would have about four hours to cool off and we would stay hidden within the wood line across the field and never be seen by unit personnel on our second visit.

One of the unwritten rules at the Mission was "Never Go Back." Once you had been seen by a unit you were trying to cover, especially if they reacted to your presence in any way, you simply got as much information as you possibly could from the first visit and left—leaving further coverage to another day. There were probably more close calls, rammings, ambushes, and injuries resulting from violation of this guideline (or variants) than any other guideline we followed. I was about to have the guideline reemphasized. Clearly the danger was that not only had we been seen, the unit now had several hours to alert all their personnel, to go over rules and plans for dealing with mission personnel, and to plan ambushes or other deterring obstacles for any follow-on visits.

Later in the day we returned to the site. The first time we had come from the south. We worked our way through a small forested area that would bring us out of the wood line directly west of the site, across the plowed field, about 150 meters to the west of the unit. My plan was to remain in the wood line and photograph the entire site from about two hundred to 250 meters away. Not as great as our aborted drive-by at a range of fifty meters but probably close enough for some good pictures.

As we got close to the edge of the wood line, I opened the top hatch of the G-Wagon and climbed on top with my Nikon ready. Smitty stopped the vehicle about thirty meters inside the wood line but still giving us a good view of the site. It was as I had hoped it would be—good light with the full complement of the unit's intercept gear deployed. Mike and Smitty began scanning the deployment with binoculars.

I was getting ready to take my first picture when I heard Mike Poindexter yell, "Get down! He's got a gun and he is going to shoot!"

Startled by Mike's yell, I heard the first bullet whiz over my head and hit a tree directly behind the G-Wagon. As I dropped back down through the top-hatch I heard two more bullets whiz by—one on either side. By this time Smitty had the vehicle in gear, and he made his second rookie mistake of the day. Rather than throwing the vehicle into reverse and backing deeper into the woods before trying to turn around, he tried to turn around where we were—leaving us momentarily broadside to the shooter (my side). Fortunately, the warrant officer with the Makarov pistol became less accurate as he emptied his pistol at us. I could still hear bullets hitting in the trees around us but none coming close enough to hear the whiz of the bullet as it passed.

We all learned some lessons that day. I broke the rule about going back again several times during my tour at the mission but only with great reluctance.

It was a rough way to start my second year, and it taught me a critical lesson. Surprisingly, it had not frightened me much—it all happened too fast. I remember a momentary surge of anger that I had no way to fight back. But as we departed the area I realized that we had been very fortunate that no one had been injured—or worse.

(As an aside, years later when I was working in Ukraine as a civilian contractor, I hired a young man to work for us who had been a Soviet lieutenant serving in the Soviet Radio Intercept Battalion in the south. We had a few laughs about being on opposite sides during the Cold War, but he told me that they considered the Radio Intercept Battalion's equipment as sensitive, and they were briefed on the activities of the three Allied Missions. Their instructions were to do what was necessary to run us off. There were no limits specified.)

• • •

I guess this might be a good segue into what our wives knew about what we were doing. USMLM reconnaissance activities were classified. Our wives did not have any clearances, nor was there a "wives eyes only" security level that would allow pillow talk about our work. But like with any human organization, people talked. Some members of the Mission were more relaxed about what they told their wives; some wives were much more curious than others.

Prior to the shooting at the comm site, I had not told my wife Dru very much about what we did in East Germany. She is a smart lady, and I am sure she figured out much about what we were doing in a general sense. But I did not want this story to get back to her somehow through the rumor-net but not have the facts straight. So we went for a walk, and I told her what happened. It was the only time that we talked about what I was doing in East Germany until Nick got killed and the classified nature of the mission was momentarily shattered. Following Nick's shooting, the details of mission activities were made very public and provided a forum for wives to question more vocally the nature of what we were doing. All she (Dru) really knew at this time was that I disappeared about twice a week into East Germany for two to four days at a time. She knew that whatever we were doing, it was classified, and that we did not sleep much and often came home filthy dirty and smelling bad. And she knew it was not a picnic.

Speaking of wives, there was a whole social side to living in Berlin that made being there very special.

First of all, the liaison function of the USMLM was real. Several times each year there were official contacts between USAREUR and GSFG. When those events occurred in East Germany, USMLM often hosted and always supported them. As a liaison officer my responsibility was normally to accompany one or two members of the US Delegation and act as an interpreter. Frankly, this was the most terrifying part of working at the mission for me. I knew that I was not a great Russian linguist and that my Russian could not sustain close observation. Or at least that was how I felt. Practically I suffered through a number of these events and got along fine. But I worried. Because political relations between the US and USSR were so poor that social interactions at both the official and unofficial level were very restricted during the four years that I was at the mission.

But I digress.

Having learned a big lesson at the comm site, I launched into my second year as a tour officer. Something else unique happened that year that I did not understand until long after. I began to join the ranks of the "old" tour officers. Every year new officers came and experienced officers left. Simply through longevity and accretion, a tour officer began to be consulted more and more about touring in East Germany simply because he had done it longer and more frequently than others. To my surprise, new tour officers began asking *me* for advice. It felt good. I liked it.

Chapter 9
The Great T-80 Chase

Sometime in my second year at USMLM, the Sovs began introducing a new tank into GSFG—the T-80. I think this is an interesting story because it taught me something about them that I would have found hard to believe if I just read about it. It demonstrated how careful they could be with security if it was important to them.

Soviets and security were two words that I found to be nearly incompatible at times, yet startlingly impressive at others. One of the things that we routinely did at the mission was to police up Soviet bivouac sites after an exercise was completed. It was incredible to us the amount of information that they could leave behind. I will concede that it was often the kind of information that you could get on US forces in West Germany if you simply subscribed to the "Stars and Stripes" newspaper, available almost everywhere that US forces were stationed in Western Europe. Nevertheless, it was classified information for them, and they left it everywhere.

On the other hand, they could move three or four divisions from their garrisons to major training areas in the vicinity of the West German border in total radio silence. We watched this happen on a number of occasions while I was at the Mission.

A typical Soviet exercise might begin with two divisions deploying from garrison to the White Horse training area on the Polish border, south and east of Berlin. The units would then move west through a series of objectives within the Alten-Grabow and Juetterbog training areas, and then near Magdeburg they would swing north to final assault sites at the Northern Elbe River crossing sites near Havel. If you straightened that line out rather than turning north at Magdeburg it put the final objective as the Rhein River in West Germany.

The first phase of the exercise would normally be a rail and road movement from the units' home garrison into one of the major training areas. This often began as a "crash-out" exercise from the home garrison. In a US unit, a "no-notice" deployment exercise began with units recalling all of their personnel (this is actually the most difficult part for most US units). Then, personnel draw weapons and prepare vehicles. Everyone lines up in a predetermined order with blackout lights on, radio silence imposed, and vehicles begin to move at the proper speed and interval between vehicles.

For Sov units, the first two hours appear to be chaos to the casual observer. Everyone lives on the garrison, so recalling personnel is not a big problem. But they consider the first two hours after notification as a period of high vulnerability. They look at their garrisons as lucrative nuclear targets. So, the objective of every Soviet unit is to get out of garrison as quickly as possible. Units assemble but there is no concern about light and noise discipline. If one or a few unit vehicles are not ready to move very quickly, they are left behind with maintenance crews and catch up to the unit in its emergency deployment site. When the unit moves, it moves quickly with lights on. If one vehicle falters at the installation gate it is immediately pushed aside and left. If it is a tank or other heavy, not-easily-moved piece of equipment and blocks the gate, a following tank or engineering vehicle might swing to one side and knock a hole through the garrison wall, and remaining vehicles exit through the new opening. The units move to predetermined emergency deployment sites several kilometers from the garrison outside of the area thought to be vulnerable to nuclear attack. Once in the deployment site, vehicles move into predetermined positions; blackout conditions and noise discipline are imposed.

The one major security measure imposed is radio silence. In the local area it may seem noisy and obvious. But to U.S. and NATO assets "listening" for indicators of an increased threat level, there is no change.

Honestly, if you understood what you are seeing, it was a thing of beauty. Less than two hours after notification, the garrisons will be empty. How do they avoid using radios when deploying? They use a system of road guides deployed in front of the units by reconnaissance units. A recon unit moving in front of the division and well-versed on the movement route will drop a soldier wearing a special uniform and helmet at every intersection at which a following unit might need to make a turn or where civilian traffic might need to be halted as a Sov column passed. As the column approaches, the "traffic regulators" (or 'TRs' as we called them) popped to attention, blocked conflicting civilian traffic, and directed the on-coming column of military equipment to the proper route. No radios, just hand signals with a white- and red-striped baton.

USMLM tour officers and NCOs loved TRs. As we patrolled our assigned areas, usually the very first sign of military exercise activity was a TR sitting on the curb or leaned against a tree at a major intersection. That immediately triggered a search for a second TR, which meant that the approaching military activity would be following the route between the two TRs and that we needed to find a good, well-hidden, observation point between the two TRs from which we could observe the military activity. Given enough time before the equipment began to move along the route, we might trace the movement route (following the line of pre-positioned TRs) for a number of kilometers in either direction, giving us more area from which to select one or more observation points.

Traffic regulators were the loneliest soldiers in the world. They might be posted as early as three days in advance of the scheduled movement with little food, no communications equipment, and no one to talk to unless there happened to be two or three at the same intersection. It could be pouring down rain or snow or subzero temperatures. They would be expected to wait. Occasionally they were put out as decoys. Regardless, it was a miserable job. All USMLM tour teams carried bags of sandwiches (I carried about forty or fifty) and packages of cigarettes (I carried about six cartons all the time). We passed them out freely to the TRs. Sometimes the TRs would talk to us and tell what was happening. More often, we just bought their silence. Regardless of what they thought or felt about USMLM tour teams, in four years I never had one TR turn down a sandwich or pack of cigarettes. The other thing that was nice about the TRs was that the last thing that happened in a column movement was that they picked up the TRs. When the TRs were picked up you knew that, at least on this route, the movement was over.

All of this to say that when the Sovs wanted it they could exercise good OPSEC when they really wanted to. Now back to the T-80.

From other sources we knew that the Soviets were introducing a new tank designated the T-80 into the Group of Soviet Forces, Germany. We began getting glimpses of the new tank. We would see a heavy-lift tractor-and-trailer unit carrying an unusually thoroughly tarped armored vehicle on the autobahn. A corner of the tarp might have torn loose, and we would get a photo of the untarped corner, and our Intel production office began putting together a composite picture of the new T-80. It became clear that in anticipation of the full-scale introduction of the tank, GSFG was giving an orientation to all of the divisions, and that was what we were seeing on the autobahns. Later during that year the introduction of the T-80 en masse to GSFG began. We still did not have a clear picture of a T-80. The Sovs began bringing them in by rail on a relatively regular schedule. They came in on several different rail lines, but when you saw them you could not mistake them for anything else. Each tank was on a separate flatcar covered with a framed tarp tent that covered the flatcar from one end to the other. The French Military Liaison Mission had a source that knew the delivery schedule, and while they did not share their source, we routinely received suggestions from FMLM to monitor this rail line or that rail line on this evening or another, and we would then stake out that rail line and count the arriving tarped rail cars.

We (the Allied Missions collectively) then followed the trains or monitored the arrival of tarped rail cars in various rail sidings, particularly in Dresden (11GTD) and Riesa (9GTD). So we knew they were coming in steadily. Yet a year passed, and we had no handheld photos of the new tank by any of the missions.

Nobody talked about it publicly, but *every* ground tour officer and NCO from all three missions wanted to be the one to get the first good handheld photos. But the Sovs were very protective, apparently restricting the movement of the tanks to nighttime and primarily within the Permanently Restricted Areas. Getting the first handheld photography of the T-80 was going to be the *"big hit"* of the year for some tour team. Every tour officer had their own ideas about how to get the hit. I spent hours sneaking around in the northern edges of the Koenigsbruek Training Area just north of the Dresden installations of the 11th Guards Tank Division. I plotted new ways in and out of the training area. When we were in one of the areas in which we knew the T-80s were deployed and took a break or nap, we parked our vehicle in the middle of tank tactical routes moving from one training area to another—my thought being that they really wouldn't run us over if they came down the trail. It was more likely that they would go around us or stop and order us out of the trail.

Either way, I planned to get a photo. Every spare moment on all of my tours was spent checking places that I thought there was a possibility of seeing a T-80 in its natural habitat. Every tour officer in all of the missions hoped to make that one big hit that would add him top the list of legendary tour officers. I was no different than the others. I wanted a big memorable hit.

At the time, Nick Nicholson was the Mission Production Officer and was carefully monitoring every report of T-80 activity; and came up with a plan to use my information about various access routes into the Koenigsbruek Training Area. He and his driver, SGT Jim McDowell, slipped into the training area under cover of darkness, found a hide for the vehicle, camouflaged the G-wagon, and spent five days physically in the training area, with Nick hiding at the edge of a major field of maneuver trying to catch the T-80. No luck.

I knew the British and French ground teams were expending similar efforts. It was a friendly competition but intense. We shared results but not tactics. Everyone wanted to be the one.

In hindsight, I think a British air team actually got the first photos. It was midnight and the tanks were moving on a bridge over an autobahn between two training areas north of Dresden. The pictures were fuzzy. But a clear ID feature of the new tank (not known at the time but clear later) were solid, deep-dish road wheels with the middle two of six road wheels set closer together than the others. At the time there was a large debate among the local experts and the judgment was that the picture was not of a T-80.

Those of us in the chase breathed a sigh of relief and went back to the hunt.

I actually think that I got the next set of pictures of a fully untarped T-80 tank. It was late November and I was with SSG John Johnson. We were staking out a rail siding at Gross Ammensleben. The rail siding was active, and we had already been close enough to know that a battalion of 18 2S3 155mm self-propelled howitzers was off-loading. It was about 0200 and I knew the route they would follow through the small East German town to their garrison just inside a nearby PRA, so we parked in the shadows on an obscure side road but with a good view of an intersection with a street light that the Artillery Battalion would pass under. At the time, our night-vision adaptors for use with our cameras were bulky and cumbersome to use. There was nothing sexy about this artillery, and with the street light we would get all of the vehicle side numbers. Before they got into the PRA we would roll up behind them to get a couple of

Vehicle Registration Numbers (VRN) from wheeled vehicles in the column. Between the side numbers and VRN we would identify the unit.

The now off-loaded vehicles began to move and passed under the street light as planned. I carefully recorded all of the side numbers from the armored vehicles.

As the end of the column approached the street light, I heard John say, "You know, it looks like there are a couple of tanks at the back of the column." I began studying them.

"They don't sound right, John," I responded. The standard Soviet tank in GSFG was the T-64. T-64s had a very distinctive sound to them. You could hear them coming for kilometers. These tanks were quiet.

"John, this is it! Those are T-80s. Let's get 'em!"

I was immediately in my camera bag trying to get my night-vision adaptor hooked up to my Nikon F3. With my night-vision adapter and my sixty-five to 185mm zoom lens attached, the camera barrel was about two feet long, and I kept banging it into the windshield.

"This isn't working," I thought to myself. So I pulled the night-vision adapter off the camera and pushed the film to ASA3200.

"John, here is what I want you to do. We are going to get out on the road behind that last tank. When I say, 'now,' you turn on every light we've got— brights, fog lights, infra-reds—everything!"

The column was past us now and rapidly approaching the metal suspension bridge that marked the edge of the PRA. The lead vehicles of the column were already crossing the bridge. We were closing fast on the last tank, but it was only one hundred meters or so from the bridge. We closed to within fifteen meters of the last tank. I could see a couple of warrant officers sitting on top of the turret.

"Okay, lights on—*now*!"

John turned on *all* the lights. The warrant officers shielded their eyes and looked at us intently. I was taking pictures as fast as I could get the shutter to function. The tanks rolled across the bridge.

John looked at me and said, "What do we do?"

"Keep going."

I knew I was getting a lot of shots of the back end of the tank but not much of the sides and certainly none of the front. We followed the column about a kilometer into the PRA without improving the photography much. Discretion set in, and we retraced our route out of the PRA. We returned to Berlin, and I turned the film in to the photo lab to be developed. I went home and got a couple of hours sleep; then went back to the office to check the photos. It was definitely the new tank with good views of the rear end. As I feared, I did not get much of the sides of the tank. So I felt like I had contributed to the T-80 mosaic that we were gradually building but not the satisfaction of "getting" the T-80.

A few days later at a Tri-Mission social function, the French team arrived full of smiles and excitement. The day before, the Chief of the FMLM Ground team, Major LeMay, had obtained broad-daylight, front, side, and rear photography of the T-80 tank driving on a tac trail north of the Koenigsbruek training area. There were congratulations and toasts all around for Major LeMay and FMLM. But I could sense it throughout the room and in my heart. A great sense of disappointment. The great T-80 chase was over.

For the Sovs, they knew we had the photos, and it was as if someone in GSFG declassified the T-80 and suddenly they were everywhere. Photos of the T-80 were a dime-a-dozen. But it had been an incredible feat in my mind. Over the course of a little more than a year the Soviets had introduced more than one thousand T-80 tanks into East Germany, geographically distributed between three divisions; and they had good enough OPSEC to deny access to the three allied liaison missions for over a year.

As an aside, ten years later working as a contractor in Ukraine, I went to visit the military museum in KIEV. There, parked in front of the museum were two tanks—one of which was a T-80. It was painted yellow with blue and pink flowers on it. It startled me that a weapon system that I had pursued so persistently over a year and a half was now relegated to a museum piece painted as if for a 1960's peace march.

I guess it is true—all glory is fleeting.

Chapter 10

2nd Year War Stories

ABS-T Engineer Training Site Wittenburg

Sometimes things just don't work out the way you have planned. I was with Smitty, and we were checking out a small engineer training area just south of Wittenburg. It was a low-key site often occupied by engineer units training on new equipment being deployed into GSFG. We were looking for the deployment of a new, tracked amphibious bridge/ferry into GSFG called the ABS-T. Not the sexiest piece of equipment in the Soviet inventory but a definite step-up in the already impressive Soviet river-crossing capabilities. As an aside, I will say that I was terribly impressed with the Soviet commitment to river-crossing training and capability. As an infantry officer, I knew that rivers were serious obstacles to ground force movement. Every bridge in Western Europe was marked with its capacity to bear weight. This isn't for the benefit of truckers hauling farm produce. It is to assist military units to use for planning military operations. As NATO forces were preparing to absorb an attack into Western Europe, they often trained not only on river-crossing operations but also on how to destroy bridges. Movies like *One Bridge Too Far* let us all remember how important bridges were to the success or failure of any military operation in Europe. On the Soviet side, planning to overcome river obstacles was built into every training exercise at every level. In East Germany, every major bridge was presumed to be targeted for destruction by NATO, and an entire replacement bridge was ready and stored nearby so that offensive operations could be quickly resumed even if a bridge is knocked out. These replacement bridges were stored in open air compounds that we kept track of and checked regularly. The facilities were so low key that no personnel were present so they were easy to check. But I was impressed that they were so prepared that they actually had replacement bridges ready to go.

But that wasn't the end of it. Every division had its own river-crossing assets, including a Pontoon Bridge company composed of eighteen bridging sections mounted on KRAZ trucks. The company always included a 19th vehicle, capable of replacing on of the truck carrying a pontoon bridge section or for extra equipment if not needed to carry a bridge section. There were also a number of amphibious, lightly-armored ferry vehicles.

Plus, the Soviet tanks all were capable of driving underwater to cross a river (after some preparation of the crossing site by engineers) using snorkels for exhaust and air. One afternoon, SSG Dave Boone and I found a good, concealed observation point near the Soviets' North Elbe Rivers Crossing Training Site and watched Soviet tank crews practice assembling and installing snorkeling kits on T-64 tanks for about five hours. They would spend about a half-hour installing the snorkeling kit; then they would hook a cable between the tank and a tank recovery vehicle. Then the tank crew would drive the tank into the river until the turret was under water. Then they would let it idle for five minutes or so. It was pretty cool to watch. The recovery vehicle was there to drag the tank back out of the river if the engine failed or something else went wrong.

But, again, I digress. All of this to explain that the Sovs took amphibious operations seriously, and we thought they might be introducing a new tracked ferry into GSFG. We were right. Smitty and I worked our way around the encampment and approached the motor pool compound from the southwest. The motor pool, we knew, was surrounded by a five-meter-high chain-link fence with only one exit—on the north side. All of the units' vehicles were parked inside the motor pool, so to chase us they would have to crank up a truck or jeep, exit through the north gate and circle the motor pool. Because we were targeting the motor pool for the new piece of equipment, if the Sovs reacted, we would see the chase vehicles start up and know exactly how much time we had to clear the area. Perfect setup. And everything went just as planned. We drove right up to the chain-link fence on the east side of the motor pool. One of the new tracked ferry vehicles was parked with its broadside facing us. I was getting good pictures, and the Sovs were slow to react. But we could see and hear several officers yelling at their men, and three trucks cranked up and headed out the gate. As the third vehicle cleared the gate, I told Smitty it was time to go. The trucks were circling the motor pool on the opposite side from us, so we had plenty of time to turn around and run the nearby dirt road to the east for a kilometer; then a quick turn to the right, five hundred meters to a railroad-crossing pole barrier where I would have to get out of the G-wagon and open/close the barrier when we drove through; then another 250 meters to a paved road, on which I knew our G-wagon could out run anything in their motor pool. I had made the escape a dozen times before without even a close call.

However, "the best laid plans of mice and men...." When we got to the rail crossing, I discovered that the rail-crossing pole barrier was locked with a lock too big for my bolt cutters. So now, what had been intended as an orderly exit from the area became a high-speed chase. We raced back for the intersection and arrived just as the three trucks raced past in front of us. They immediately saw us and began apply the brakes to get turned around. We shot across the intersection behind them and raced north on the dirt road. I thought, "we are safe; they will never catch us now."

But as I looked in the rearview mirror, I could see that two of the trucks were coming fast. "Too late," I thought to myself, "we were going to get away".

Suddenly the smooth-graded dirt road we were running at one hundred KPH stopped being a paved road and turned into a Soviet tank trail. Tanks tended to create deep ruts and gullies in their tank trails. This was no exception. The dirt road dipped into a quick series of deep gullies each about twenty to thirty meters from peak to peak, and each about eight to ten feet high. We hit the first dip going about one hundred KPH. As we dipped into the gully, I could see that we were going way too fast to stay smoothly in the rut. We hit the upside of the gully, and the G-wagon launched into the air. I could hear Smitty cursing while I was hanging on to the dashboard thanking God that I had my seatbelt on. The G-Wagon came down hard. I thought the tires were going to blow, and it felt like my guts had all shaken loose inside my body. But the tires held and after a few minutes my guts began to settle back into place. Smitty kept control of the G-Wagon, and in a few minutes the trucks stopped trying to catch us. Not exactly how I planned our departure, but we made it without getting caught.

Jaennersdorf Tank Range

Another time, I was with John Johnson. Our target was the Jaennersdorf Tank Range north of Berlin—almost always occupied. We were watching for evidence that the Sovs were training to use a depleted uranium projectile from their tanks' main guns. The range paralleled a main road, so was ideal for watching. The range was offset from the main road about one hundred meters, so it was possible to run down the road and turn in in a number of places to get to the edge of the tank range. You had to be careful because, for safety reasons, the Sovs would run a patrol alongside of the range before they began to fire. Of course, if the safety patrol saw one of our vehicles they would report it, and they would make a concerted effort to run us off before they began firing. So the idea was to slip in to the edge of the range just after the safety patrol passed by; then watch the firing exercise. My plan was to get there and slip into the woods and wait for the safety patrol; then go to the edge of the range as soon as they were gone.

We got to Jaennersdorf just after first light and moved to the edge of the range to see what was going on. T-64 tanks were moving into position on the firing line, but I could tell that they were running behind schedule and would not begin firing for a couple of hours. We were too exposed on the edge of the range so I told John to back out and go across the main road to a forested area on the south side of the road. I figured that we could get a couple of hours of sleep and then sneak back in for another look.

I woke up an hour later and could see civilian vehicles driving by on the main road. I knew that we were too exposed and had probably been seen. I shook Jonh awake and said we needed to move. Unfortunately, I was right. We had been seen, and Sovs were busy blocking every exit from the wooded area with a truck. We began racing down dirt roads and trails trying to find an unblocked exit.

The Sovs sent several trucks into the forest to try to flush us out. For the next thirty minutes, I felt like I was in an episode of the *Keystone Cops* as we raced one way and the Sovs another; us trying to escape, them trying to pin us in. We could see them running through the woods sometimes on intersecting roads with near misses at the intersection. Speeds were fast enough to throw us airborne in small jumps occasionally. Over the next thirty minutes with a dozen close calls, we finally made it through the forested area to a plowed field, and John drove straight across it to a paved road on the opposite side, and we departed the area.

Not exactly the way I planned it.

East German SA-5 Site

Normally I had no desire to do air team targets, frankly because I wasn't very good at Air Craft ID; but for a while the air team was short on experienced tour personnel, so I was tapped to do some back-seating with some of their new trainees. I was tagged to go out with Major Skip Bohn, designated to be the future chief of the air team. He lived right up the street from me; and his wife Peggy and my wife had become good friends. Skip was a funny guy; I thought it might be fun. The air team was short of drivers at the time so they were also borrowing ground team drivers. So, not only was I back-seating, Smitty was driving. We figured it was almost as good as having a ground team in the area. It was a running joke in all of the missions that for an air team to encounter a ground target such as a vehicle column was almost pointless, as the vehicle identification sounded something like, "big truck, big truck, little truck, little truck, armored vehicle with big gun, armored vehicle, no gun," and so on. I will say that they were pretty good with cameras and often re-deemed themselves with their photography. All this to say that having two ground guys in the car substantially increased the value of any information re-covered during air team encounters with ground targets. Skip was a sharp guy and ready to make his mark as an air team guy, so I figured he would not want or need much advice from a ground guy anyhow. He gave me a quick rundown on his target list the afternoon before we departed so I would know what we were trying to accomplish; and with that, we were ready.

I didn't really like doing East German targets for several reasons: first, the So-viets never let the East Germans have the latest or best equipment, so you weren't going to get a good report on Warsaw Pact on something sexy at an East German facility. Second, while East German populace disliked the Soviets and frequently would point out the locations of Sov units if such units were in the area. *However,* if the East German populace thought that our target was an East German unit, they were much more likely to report your presence to the local Volkespolizei.

Finally, East German soldiers were much more alert and reacted to our tour vehicles more aggressively than Soviet soldiers. So, in my mind, East German Units were of lower value than Soviet sites, while of significantly greater risk.

Nevertheless, Skip's first target of the day was an East German SA-5 site up near Rostock. While not sexy, upgrading East German air defenses to SA-5s was a significant upgrade. We already knew the upgrade was in progress. Skip's task was simply to check the status of the upgrade.

The SA-5 site was under construction and did not have a full complement of troops yet, so Skip's plan was pretty simple. We would just drive up to the front gate of the facility; he would stand on top of the G-wagon and look over the gate. That was how the air team had been handling this facility for the last six months. We were going to hit the site near first light, so, odds were, in my opinion, this would probably would work given what Skip expected to see.

As luck would have it, however, as we approached the facility's main gate, Smitty suddenly cursed and swerved left into a farmer's field, saying something about a soldier on a motorcycle. I glanced out of the back window of the G-wagon and saw an East German soldier on a military motorcycle with a rifle slung across his back trying to follow us across the farmer's field. He obviously knew who we were and was after us. As I watched, he lost his balance in the field and went down. He did not appear to be injured, and as he rose from the dirt, he was pulling his rifle from his shoulder. Skip made a good decision and told Smitty to get us out of there. We would move on to the next target. Later that day, Skip decided to go back.

I reminded him about the "never go back" rule. But he was sure that he knew a route that was safe. And, in fact, it was a fairly obscure route. We crossed through a farmer's field to a gate that led to a trail that paralleled the installation back fence. There was a steep gully to our right.

As the trail became narrower and the gully deeper, I told Skip I thought we had gone about as far as we should go. Skip reluctantly agreed and told Smitty to back up and get us out of there. As we retraced our path to the farmer's field, we saw three East German military dump trucks (Zil-555) enter the field from the opposite side. They split up so that they could come at us from head on and both sides. They were coming fast, and Smitty headed directly for the middle truck intending to by-pass him before he could get turned. The two flanking trucks were coming fast. We were moving pretty fast, but there was a ditch in the middle of the field. Smitty yelled "Hold on!" and we hit the ditch going full speed. I was the only one in the vehicle without a seat belt, and my shoulders hit the roll-bar on the ceiling. As we jumped the ditch, the dump truck coming from my side just missed ramming us and passed to our rear. Smitty zigzagged passed the center truck, and we raced to the main road. All three trucks recovered and followed us for a half-hour until we had cleared the area.

Wow! How many times did I need to learn this lesson? NEVER GO BACK!

Chapter 11

2nd Year (Continued) War Stories

Riesa Bivouac Site

Since it was not far off the main road south from Berlin, tour teams were routinely tasked to check the Riesa Bivouac Site. Various types of activity was routinely reported there, such as engineer units and armored units from the 9th Guards Tank Division conducting river-crossing training at the southern Elbe river-crossing site. Communications units also deployed to the training area. Personally, I had checked the biv site many times and never seen anything. So, one overcast fall day when I was headed south with SSG Ron Blake driving, I looked up the hill toward the site and saw several R404/414 relay antennas extending above the tree line—I was very excited. I wanted to check the tree line out from another angle and knew it was possible to get fairly close coming from the south, so I had Ron continue south for another two kilometers on the main road. Then, we drove west to the base of a bald hill located directly to the south of the biv site. Sometimes the Sovs posted a vehicle/guard on the hill for security, but this day there were no security vehicles. It was around 1100, and the sky was gray and overcast but no rain. Cautiously we moved toward the crest of the hill but remained in defilade on the back side of the hill.

We moved forward just enough to see a communications unit begin to emerge from the forested area of the bivouac site into the open field between the forest and our position. About forty or fifty vehicles emerged from the forest and set up right in front of us. About half of the vehicles were BTR-60 armored transporters heavily modified with antennas and communications equipment. The remainder were light and medium Box Bodied Vehicles (BBV) (GAZ-66 light trucks and ZIL-131 and Ural-375 medium trucks), also heavily modified.

Ron and I watched, and I shot up a couple of rolls of 35mm film while we watched the deployment unfold. The temperature was mild, so we had the windows rolled down on the G-Wagon. As I loaded my third roll of film in my NIKON F3, I glanced in the vehicle's external rearview mirror and was startled to see two Soviet soldiers crawling through the grass toward the vehicle from about twenty meters behind us. I shouted at Ron to get us out of here. As I yelled at Ron, the two soldiers jumped to their feet with rifles with fixed bayonets and raced the last twenty meters toward the G-Wagon.

The standard time for going from low-key observation mode to high-speed escape mode for mission drivers was about one second; and as I rolled up the window on my side, Ron had the G-Wagon rolling. With the soldiers behind us, there was only one direction for us to go and that was straight forward toward the deployment.

Vehicles were still emerging from the forest, and we were seen immediately. We could have tried running along the crest of the hill, but the ground was rough and uneven, giving the Sovs an advantage with their cross-country vehicles. Ron did not hesitate but charged straight ahead into and through the deployment. BTR-60s do not have a tight-turning radius, so we had our chance to get away as five or six of them tried to turn to chase us. We shot through the deployment to hit and turn left on a good dirt road that paralleled the southern edge of the forest. It looked like it was going to be close.

We were quick enough to evade most of the pursuing vehicles, but the vehicles on the west side of the deployment site were better positioned to cut us off. Two of the BTR-60s had taken good angles across the open field but underestimated our speed. They both pulled onto the road, having just missed their best opportunity to ram us; but they were in good enough position to hit the road behind us and follow us. Another five hundred meters and we were on a paved road rapidly accelerating away from them. But our troubles were not over yet.

The paved road we were on headed directly into a Permanently Restricted Area about two kilometers in front of us, and no significant roads to turn on to get away from the still following BTR-60s. On a paved road the BTR-60s could not match our speed, so we accelerated to gain some separation. Just at the edge of the PRA, we entered a small village; the road curved, and we lost visual contact with the BTR-60s (and they lost contact with us). Ron quickly turned into a farmer's barnyard, and we stopped behind the barn. We sat quietly behind the barn and watched the BTR-60s race by; then we pulled out behind them and sped away in the opposite direction. The crew in the armored vehicles saw us emerge from the barnyard, so they quickly turned around to continue the pursuit. But their hearts were no longer in the game, so after following us for another three or four kilometers to be sure we were actually leaving the area, they broke off the chase and returned to the bivouac site, and we continued south on Route 2 to our next target.

First Serious Detention
Northern Elbe River Crossing Site

It was about midway through my second year that I was finally detained. I was with SSG John Johnson, and we were tasked to cover part of a major river-crossing training exercise involving at least two divisions from GSFG. Often, river-crossing exercises of this size were so big that the three missions drew up special boundaries, and all three missions sent teams to cover the exercise. Such was the case with this exercise, and it had already been going on for about five days. Paul Nelson and my driver SSG Johnson had been there on the first day of the exercise and detained on east side of the river.

I arrived on the fifth day of the exercise and was covering the west side of the river. This was all near the small town of Havel. Normally the GSFG staff would have issued a Temporary Restricted Area (TRA) notice, but for some reason they had not done so, which, by Mission rules, allowed us to be there. John and I had run tac trails and back roads to get into the area without being noticed—often following tactical units into the area as they deployed.

There was so much activity that nearly each direction that we turned we encountered another unit. Tanks, armored personnel carriers, self-propelled and towed artillery, air defense systems, POL and ammo trucks—it was all there. In the morning on our second day, it appeared that the exercise was over, and we began to try to get out of the area. This turned out to be more complicated than I anticipated. We were so deep inside of the exercise that no matter which way we turned we encountered military equipment blocking the roads. We finally found a small paved road that looked promising. We ran about two kilometers and encountered a couple of squads of soldiers shoveling mud that tanks had dragged up on the paved road The soldiers recognized us as a USMLM team as we drove past and were yelling at us. I did not notice the two lieutenants with the squad. We drove another half kilometer and encountered a four-way intersection. It didn't look good. There were trucks and armored vehicles for as far as we could see on all three of the other roads leading away from the intersection—one column of which we had already run that morning. I decided to go back and find another way out. I told John to turn around.

As we approached the squad we had passed earlier, they now lined both sides of the road and were waving their shovels as if to hit the G-wagon. It looked bad, but I told John to keep going. I didn't think they would really try to hit us with the shovels. What I didn't notice was that the last person on each side of the road was a lieutenant—in any army, unpredictable. The lieutenant on my side of the road cranked his shovel back like a baseball bat and swung it toward the windshield. He let it go and it crashed into the windshield. The windshield exploded and glass went everywhere. I could see the lieutenant on John's side was about to do the same, so I yelled for him to stop. We had not been going very fast as we passed the soldiers, so the vehicle immediately stopped. We sat motionless for a couple of minutes trying to figure out if the glass had cut us anywhere. Although we were covered in small shards of glass, it did not appear that we were actually cut, so we began shaking shards of glass from our uniforms.

The lieutenant on my side of the vehicle approached and looked through the now smashed windshield. I leaned forward and told him (in Russian) that he had just violated an international agreement between the United States and the Soviet Union and was in serious trouble. He said there was a military exercise in progress and we should not be there. I reminded him that if that was the case, his headquarters would have issued a TRA and they had not. As we sat there, military vehicles began passing, and they attempted to obscure our vision by placing a canvas cover from one of their trucks over our vehicle. In about forty-five minutes a captain arrived on the scene (I presumed the lieutenant's commander). He looked through the windshield at me and said, "This is really bad." He walked away, and I could see and hear him chewing the lieutenant out. I heard him conclude with, "And you can stay here until the Kommandatura arrives!"

About two hours later, a major from the Kommandatura office in Havel arrived. I could see the lieutenant brighten as it looked like someone had arrived that might sympathize with him. But as the major approached the vehicle, he recognized John as having been with the team that had been detained earlier in the week and reached through the windshield, shaking John's hand and greeting him by name. The lieutenant was crestfallen.

That was not quite the end of it. As usual, they prepared an AKT and showed it to me but did not ask for a signature. Then, to get us quickly out of the area, they ferried us across the river in a GPS ferry, and we drove south back to Potsdam on Route 5. It was January and not a lot of fun without a windshield.

North Elbe River Crossing Site—Again

One other time I was with Smitty, and we were tasked to go to the North Elbe site—only this time we were the first team to arrive. We came in late at night, running a tac trail from the southwest. We could tell something was going on because the tac trail was already chewed up pretty badly by armored vehicles of some type. I knew the trail pretty well and knew that it went clear down to one of the prepared river-crossing sites. We were running the trail with infrared headlights and our night-vision goggles and drove to a clearing about one kilometer from the river-crossing site. There was a farmhouse and a barn about halfway across the clearing, so we pulled into the barnyard and parked behind the barn. It was a bright moonlit night—almost like daylight—and we could see any movement on the tac trail clearly.

Almost as soon as we settled in behind the barn, regiments of BMPs (tracked armored personnel carriers) began running down the trail toward the river. As they passed we could hear them deploying into small clumps of trees not far from the river. They would pull in, then we could hear them positioning the vehicles for a short while and then they would go quiet—waiting for the scheduled morning river-crossing exercise.

It was great for Smitty and me. Because of the brightness of the moon we could clearly see everything running along the tac trail. However, as the third regiment began to pass our barn, a BMP broke down exactly on the opposite side of the barn. The rest of the regiment moved on, but we could clearly hear the crew of the broken down BMP talking. All it was going to take for them to find us was for someone to walk around the back of the barn to take a leak. We heard a truck arrive with a repair crew, and we could hear them banging on the BMP as they tried to get it working. We sat for nearly an hour—Smitty with his hand on the ignition key the whole time.

After about an hour we heard the BMP finally start, and after a little more yelling they moved on down the tac trail. We were lucky that no one ever walked around to the back of the barn. By this time the tac trail was clear, and it did not appear that any move units were moving in, so we got on the trail and moved about half a kilometer closer to the river-crossing site. I wanted to be closer to the river before first light so we could possibly watch the actual river crossing, but it seemed that every small clump of trees from half a kilometer out down to the river had tanks or BMPs parked in them.

We moved further to the northwest and finally found a spot to rest but close enough to the river to move in for the exercise. It was about 0330 when we finally stopped. I thought we might sleep a little, but we were too keyed up and too vulnerable. So we sat and waited. In the darkness we could hear surprisingly little considering that there were, by my estimation, probably at least two tank regiments and three motorized rifle regiments nearby.

Precisely at 0530 we heard tanks begin to crank their engines and warm up. We began moving toward a nearby break in the river dikes. Once inside I knew we would be able to see the actual river-crossing site. As we penetrated the dike, I could hear the tanks begin moving. I could see a row of five or six T-64 tanks in the early morning fog with their snorkels up moving toward the river. I also saw a BRDM-2 scout vehicle parked about one hundred meters from the break in the dike—obviously for security. He saw us, and Smitty saw the BRDM-2 at about the same moment. Smitty did a quick U-turn, and the Scout vehicle started after us. As we spun around, I could see a second row of T-64 tanks emerge from the fog headed to the river. It was really a pretty site—all of those tanks rolling through the fog with their snorkels up. It would have been great to be able to watch them enter the river and snorkel across, but it was not to be. Smitty and I spent the next hour trying to evade the security vehicles that chased us northwest out of the area.

Chapter 12

Sovs

I came to respect the Soviet forces in ways that I did not expect. In later assignments as an arms control inspector under the Intermediate Nuclear Forces (INF) Treaty and Strategic Arms Reduction Treaty (START), I was able to visit many Soviet (and later, Russian) military bases and to see them under much less stressful (less for me) conditions; and often wondered to myself how a nation that had such a terrible national and local utilities system (particularly plumbing and electricity) could pose a realistic threat to the United States. But I have to say, they did some things well.

They built good, soldier-proof weapons systems. One of their strengths and weaknesses was that they taught there soldiers to perform specific tasks. If the soldier was a machine gunner, he was taught to fire a machine gun. The weapon itself would function. I think everyone who is familiar with military things is familiar with the reliability of the AK-47 rifle. That reliability was built into every weapons system. But it wasn't just the weapons that impressed me. It was their approach to military activity that was unique. Our soldiers were cross-trained in everything. The Sovs were dealing with an all draftee army with all of the morale, discipline, and motivational issues that come with an all draftee army. In the twenty-four months that they had him, if they could make that soldier good at his primary function that was good enough. It led them to practical, low-key approaches to various activities. A few examples of their simple straight forward approaches:

Unattended Repeater Stations

One problem every military force is confronted with is survivability of command and control systems. Everyone on the battlefield is trying to identify and destroy command units. A headless army is ineffective. Armies are all reliant on radio for communications to one degree or another. Radio signals are subject to intercept and, when located, subject to attack. The Sovs were very practical about their solution to this. They had built an elaborate system of underground lines and repeater stations throughout East Germany that as divisions moved into the forward area rather than rely entirely on radio transmissions; their major units could tap into this underground system and communicate using more secure hard-wired systems.

During my second year, I was tasked during one tour to visit and photograph as many URS as possible. It was on a day that we switched areas from Area A to C, so I started in the North near Rostock and finished up about midnight the next day near Dresden. Altogether I probably hit forty URS. Frankly it was a pretty low-key (boring) trip. It was a bit of a challenge finding them, as usually I had only a map grid coordinate the precision of which depended on whoever had discovered the URS in the first place. Once I got to the general vicinity, they were not hard to find. The URS itself was always underground, but the entrance was a cone of earth topped by a circular hatch about the size of the top of a fifty-five gallon drum or a little larger. Surprisingly none of them were locked, although I quickly discovered that many of them had what appeared to be a detent pin that triggered an alarm. I didn't worry about alarms too much because they were generally in remote locations, and I didn't stay at any one of them long enough for anyone to react. A few had barbed-wire enclosures around the earth cone, but I couldn't see anything inside them that made them seem special or different from the others (more on this in a minute). It did occur to me as I moved from Rostock south checking URS's that, if they were alarmed and being monitored by anyone in a central location, I was setting myself up for an ambush somewhere in the south as I worked my way down.

Each URS was about three meters in diameter, usually containing a bank (or two) of repeaters and plug in points. Some appeared to be pressurized. I just noted the nomenclature and photographed everything. Several times I found URS that had equipment hooked into them. In one case I followed wires coming from the URS for a number of kilometers until it turned into a Permanent Restricted Area. In another case I found wires running several hundred meters to an R-404/R414 relay set.

All of the above to say that the Sovs preparations to move through East Germany while minimizing their radio signature impressed me.

Road Guides/Traffic Regulators (TR)
Another aspect of moving units without a radio signature was the use of Road Guides or Traffic Regulators. Rather that counting on lead units to navigate on their own, the Sovs used a system of Road Guides to keep their units moving fast and on the right route. Recon units would precede the main body on any move—sometimes a day or more in advance—placing road guides at key intersections to guide units to make a turn or take a specific route if an intersection might be confusing. Wearing white helmets with a red band around the top, white gloves, and brandishing a baton painted white with red or black bands on it, road guides would pop to attention as columns approached and direct their movement along the correct route. In peace time traffic regulators became a key tip off to mission personnel of an impending road movement. When we found one, we looked for another and positioned ourselves between them to monitor the approaching column as it passed. Of course the Sovs knew we did this and would sometimes put out false positions to mislead us, but we were pretty good at finding the real route. We also knew that if the Sovs were really going to war we would simply be swept aside and never heard from again.

But, again, what impressed me was this simple approach to moving large units with almost no radio transmissions.

Crash-Out Exercises
When a US unit responds to an alert notification, we go through an elaborate drill of getting all personnel into the barracks, vehicles lined up, black-out lights on, all equipment and vehicles accounted for; and when everything is ready, we move out with all vehicles, moving at the proper speed, maintaining the proper distance between vehicles, and everything done in radio silence. It looks good, and commanders at all levels within an organization are graded on how well they get it all done and whether or not they get it done on time. I think the Sovs take a more practical approach. They presume that every garrison location is known to NATO and thus is potentially a lucrative nuclear target. So their approach is to get everything out of garrison as quickly as

possible. Don't worry for the first couple of hours while you are trying to clear the garrison about light and noise discipline, just get out. Most garrisons have a couple of rally points that units move to during the emergency deployment. Most of the soldiers—drivers especially—know where the emergency deployment locations are; so as units assemble, as soon as the bulk of the unit is ready, they move, leaving broken-down vehicles behind and abandoning any vehicle that has an accident or ceases running for any reason. Maintenance personnel remain behind and get the vehicle running as soon as the vehicle is running the driver continues to the designated emergency deployment site.

On arrival at the initial deployment site (five or ten kilometers from the garrison) in many cases, there are predesignated parking spots for each vehicle. Drivers know where their spots are, and even repaired vehicles move directly to them. Once they have cleared the garrison and are no longer perceive themselves as such a lucrative nuclear target, they go to full light and noise discipline and begin their deployment in good order. It is a fascinating activity to watch. All kinds of noise and lights as they are trying to clear the garrison followed by a much more disciplined movement from their emergency deployment site. Vehicles that stall or have other problems are simply bypassed.

What I am trying to say is that for a country that could not get electricity effectively delivered to all of its citizens or that could not build a decent plumbing system, they still did military things well. And often they did things that looked inefficient to us but that had good logic to it. I did not appreciate this at first, but somewhere during my second year it began to make sense.

Chapter 13
Junior Year

New Chief of Mission

The arrival of Colonel Roland Lajoie more or less marked the beginning of my "junior" year. He arrived from Moscow, where he had been serving as Army Defense Attaché. I was learning that this Soviet foreign area officer crowd was a pretty tight-knit inbred group. COL Lajoie already knew about half our tour officers and was thoroughly familiar with USMLM and what we did. He was very commonsensical, and I came to admire his style of management (which was good because I worked for him three times during my Army career).

In order to get a feel for how tour officers conducted themselves in the field, he scheduled himself to backseat with each of us several times. Two incidents come to mind from that first tour with the colonel.

First, SSG Ron Blake was my driver. I liked touring with Ron because we had good "karma." When we toured something exciting always seemed to happen. As we prepped for the tour, I told Ron in no uncertain terms that he would take instructions from me and not COL Lajoie if things got hot. I didn't want any confusion in a tight situation. Ron was okay with that. It proved important later on.

I think I made my first good impression on COL Lajoie when I briefed him on the mission—what our route would be, targets and what we would do at each, special security concerns, equipment that I would be taking, and so on. It wasn't anything special, I just briefed him on my normal plan. But it was thorough.

Later that same evening, we had our first bit of excitement. We were moving toward a target that we were going to cover after dark, and a UAZ-469 (Sov Jeep) with four officers on board took a special interest in us and began following us. We made a couple of small efforts to shake them, which only seemed to provoke them. In order to move on, we were going to have to do something more aggressive. I told Ron to try to lose them. He sped up to about one hundred KPH, and as we drove into the middle of a small town we switched off the main lights and went to infrared with our night-vision goggles. The UAZ had fallen behind a couple hundred meters. In the center of town, we turned right, and COL Lajoie told Ron to turn and hide behind a large building on the right. I told Ron to keep going out of town. Ron kept going. Just outside of town there was an open gate with a trail into a plowed field. I told Ron to hit that trail and drive to the middle of the field. We stopped there and waited. Ron began apologizing to the colonel for not turning where he said to turn; but as we waited and watched in the darkness, we saw the UAZ pass the field on the road. COL Lajoie told Ron not to worry about it—I was the one in charge. I liked his style.

COL Lajoie made it clear to us that, while he did not intend to sharpshoot our actions on the road, he did intend to monitor our activities. What we were doing was too sensitive and dangerous to go without question. I got a taste of that firsthand when, during one of our periods of "walking on eggshells," I had a fairly close call with an East German unit.

Our guidance on this occasion was that we were to get no closer to any Sov or East German unit than half a kilometer. I was out with SSG Jesse Schatz, southwest of Dresden. We were transiting an area en route from one site to another, running back roads to avoid surveillance. We were climbing a steep hill, and, as the road crested the hill, we encountered an East German unit dressed in full MOP gear and running a good-sized chemical decontamination exercise. They had all of their special decontamination equipment set up and attached to their vehicles. We were clearly within half a kilometer. The unit was stretched along the side of the road; we were on not more than thirty meters away from the road.

Jesse said, "What do you want to do?"

The personnel were not reacting to us at all, clearly distracted by the protective gear that they were wearing. No one was even looking at us. So I picked up my grab camera and told Jesse to drive past the unit slowly unless someone started to react. So we drove by the unit at about twenty KPH, and I got good photos of the whole thing. We departed without incident.

We returned to Berlin. I filled out my highlight report and turned the film in for processing and went home to get some sleep. When I came in the next morning, I was asked to step into COL Lajoie's office. It was not unusual for tour officers to be asked to debrief the colonel on a recent mission, so I was more or less expecting it. When I came in, he had the stack of photos of the chemical decontamination exercise on his desk.

He said, "This is some pretty neat stuff, Tom; tell me about it."

So we started through the photos in the order taken. I was telling him what the unit had been doing and the lack of reaction to our presence. I was tap-dancing around the fact that we were only about thirty meters away from them when the colonel tossed the last photo on the table, in which I had managed to capture the G-wagon's right side rear-view mirror, in which could easily be seen my hands holding a camera, and, on the other side of the mirror, an East German soldier about fifteen meters from the G-wagon; at which point I was forced to confess that we were a lot closer than guidance permitted.

As an example of his approach, I explained what happened and my decision to take advantage of the situation. At this point I was an experienced tour officer reacting to an unforeseen situation, and I was correct in my judgment of the probable outcome. Colonel Lajoie accepted that. He never stopped second-guessing us, but I always felt that it was so he would more nearly understand what was going on when something did go bad. I think his approach made him about as ready to handle the situation when Nick Nicholson was killed at Ludwigslust as was humanly possible.

The colonel paid the price for touring with each of the tour officers. He spent enough time on the road that he was caught in a bad incident while backseating with Major Rich Lyons (the Road Warrior). They were involved in an incident in the local area in which their G-wagon was rammed and his cheek bone was chipped. It gave him an up-close-and-personal sense of what his tour officers and NCOs encountered every day.

Chapter 14
More Stories

Warsaw Pact Logistics Exercise in the Genthin Gap

One of the games we played with the Sovs, since we had no radios, was that if a set of exercise related Temporary Restricted Area notifications were received while a tour team was on the road, the Sovs could not hold them accountable for violating the TRA because they did not know it was in place. Taking advantage of this theme, we would sometimes try to catch a returning team before they returned to the Potsdam House. If successful we would give them the boundaries of the TRA and then send them in to check it out.

I was returning with SGT Charles Smith from a long tour in Area A, including targets around Rostock, and Smitty and I were both tired. As we ran south along Route 5 back to Berlin, we saw another USMLM Vehicle. It was the Ground Operations Officer, John Eschrich, and SFC Hans Tiffany. They had a load of sandwiches and cokes for us and new instructions. The Sovs had issued a TRA notice for an area we referred to as the Genthin Gap, and we were to turn around and check it out over the next twelve to twenty-four hours.

Like I said, Smitty was beat, so I told him to get some sleep and I would drive for a while. As we started into the Genthin Gap, we began to encounter vehicle columns of increasing size. The interesting thing was that these columns were fuel and ammo trucks from Poland and Czechoslovakia mixed in with similar Soviet columns. The further we went, the larger the columns got. The Czechs and the Poles did not know us, so they were not reacting at all; but the Soviet units did, and as they began to react, I decided it was time to get Smitty back into the driver's seat. It was just dusk as Smitty and I swapped, and we had no more than gotten back into the G-wagon when a Kommandatura GAZ-66 turned the corner behind us—clearly after us. We immediately raced down the nearest paved road. GAZ-66s were fast—fast enough to keep up with us, so we knew we had to lose this one. We killed the lights and put on our night-vision goggles and turned on the IR headlights. I thought I saw a vehicle parked off to the side of the road on our right. Within a few minutes, it was clear why—we were running headlong into a Czech-motorized rifle unit of some size. Smitty turned to the right into a plowed field, made a large loop, and crossed the road we had been on before; and drove directly into the middle of the field across on the other side. We drove to the middle of the field, where we promptly sank to our axles in mud. Smitty killed the engine, and we watched for the next hour while the Kommandatura GAZ-66 and several other vehicles ran the roads around us, shining their headlights into the fields on both sides of the road trying to spot us. After about an hour, they stopped actively searching for us—us having once again maintained the mythological capability of Mission teams to simply disappear.

We were still in the open field when the river-crossing exercise started. We could tell even being four or five kilometers away by the noise of the tank and armored personnel carrier engines—probably one or two regiments. But more impressively to me, they began firing illumination rounds from their artillery. It started at about 0030, and for the next five hours, they kept at least six rounds in the air above the river-crossing site—in essence conducting a five-hour-daylight river-crossing in the darkest part of the night.

Around 0300 we managed to get free of the mud in the middle of the field, and we began trying to work our way down to the river-crossing site, but it was impossible. Nothing was moving. There were just hundreds of trucks parked alongside of every road leading down to the river. Around 0500 supply and fuel trucks began leaving the area, and by dawn most of the vehicles were gone.

I don't like to criticize something that I could only see parts of, but it looked to me as if only a few of the thousand trucks we counted actually delivered anything. But I suppose that just getting a thousand supply and fuel trucks from three or four countries moving at one time was impressive. And the five-hour illumination round display was impressive. But I kept thinking all night about what a handful of US Special Forces soldiers or Rangers could have done to disrupt the exercise if it had been for real.

Rostock

Speaking of Rostock (where Smitty and I were returning from before we were turned around to go into the TRA near Genthin), that could be a very interesting tour. First of all, all of the Soviet air defense units went to Rostock once per year to do live fire training at a range on the coast of the Baltic Sea. They always off-loaded at the same rail siding, so with the volume of activity, there was almost always something in the rail siding to observe. Mostly I had seen SA-9 and SA-13 missile systems in the rail siding. You had to be careful because it was a narrow siding and easy to get ambushed in. Because we checked it so often, the rail yard staff watched for us and alerted the Sovs when they saw us. One time when I was there with Steve Eairhardt, we saw a train full of SA-13s and were waiting to get good photos, but for some reason they were taking their time; so we pulled back into the forest alongside the tracks to take a nap. We woke up a half hour later to find soldiers being dropped off along the wood line on two sides of us and a truck load headed to a third side. Fortunately, we woke up before they could really set their trap, and we cleared the area smartly.

The other really interesting thing about Rostock was the port facility. There were always a good number of Soviet vessels in the port, and there were several good vantage points from which to observe them. I was not so familiar with the port because most of the Russian fleet coverage was done by our resident Marine, LTC Larry Kelley. Larry probably knew more about the Rostock port facility than anyone else in all three allied missions; so, for my one trip there, I sat down with him to get a thorough briefing. The biggest problem with covering the naval facilities was that it was done best from the northeast side of the port. In order to get there, you had to go onto a peninsula for which there was only one road in and out; so if you were seen going in (high probability) and they wanted to do it, they could easily catch you trying to go out. It was a major highway, so blocking it was a disruption to normal business, so unless you did something very provocative it was unlikely that they would make the effort.

I was going there with Jesse Schatz who had been there with Larry several times, so at least he had been there and was generally familiar with all of the targets we were tasked to cover.

Our major task was to take a look at one specific dock where new equipment being deployed to GSFG were often offloaded. It was most easily seen from the opposite side of the bay, so we crossed into the one-way in and out Peninsula. By the target folder and Larry's guidance, the best vantage point was the shoreline directly opposite the dock. The observation points were set at the end of three narrow trails through a series of garden plots. The trails left from the same paved road more or less like the spokes on a wheel. We headed down one of the spokes and arrived at the edge of the bay directly across the bay from the dock of interest. A ship was at the dock, but we could not see anything on the deck or being offloaded. What we had not noticed, as we left the paved road down the small trail through the garden plots, was that two busloads of cadets from a nearby naval academy had noticed us and stopped to block our exit back onto the paved road. As we started back up the path, a dozen or so cadets were out of the buses and blocking the path.

We backed up and began working our way through garden plots toward the next path back to the main road, only to discover that the cadets had discovered this path as well and blocked it also. Jesse did some highly-acrobatic driving (we nearly tipped over at one point) but managed to get to the third access path which the cadets had not found. As we pulled up on the paved road, the cadets saw us and all rushed for their buses. We were finished with our tasks for Rostock, so we headed back through the one road egress from the peninsula. The cadets were clearly having a good time and followed us in their buses until we left the Rostock city limits.

I only remember seeing one major exercise in Northern East Germany and that was only during the return phase. The Sovs had declared a large Temporary Restricted Area during the dates which they expected the exercise to run, but either the dates had changed and they did not remember to change the dates on the TRA notification, or the exercise was taking longer to close out than anticipated; because when we (Hans Tiffany and me) arrived, there were still traffic regulators everywhere and units were still lined up at rail sidings trying to load up. It appeared that we were going to be able to cover everything as it went home. The terrain in the area was low rolling hills covered with grain crops—most recently harvested—with occasional small clumps of forest to hide in. We tried several spots and settled on one that was close to a highway with traffic regulators posted, but which also allowed us to observe a rail line leading directly out of one of the load out points. It was near perfect.

It was close enough to the highway that, once it got dark, we would be able to move to a spot along the road where we could easily inventory units moving down that road. The rail line was close enough to our hide that we would not have to move to inventory units moving by rail; we could get vehicle markings from our hide as well as good photos without having to move at all. I think it must be a universal feature of all armies that, when it is time to go home, all of those good operational security measures that you practiced when deploying seem to get tossed out when you are headed home. So where we would have probably been chased off had these units been deploying, now that they were leaving, we were pretty much being ignored. We inventoried six or eight train-loads of equipment moving by rail and several road columns.

We were in the middle of an active farming community, and before long we were noticed by neighborhood kids and there were about fifteen of them on bicycles surrounding us. It didn't take them long to make the connection between the columns and trains with military equipment and our presence. They bombarded us with questions about America, about our families, about the G-wagon—anything they could think of. We tried to get them to leave— I could just see us needing to depart in a hurry with fifteen kids surrounding us. We relocated twice in hopes that the kids would get bored and leave us alone. No luck; they found us both times and stayed around until near mid-night. But we got what we needed. When we left for good, I thought about giving them all some sandwiches and cokes, but decided if we had to come back to this area it would just encourage them to bother us more in the future, So I let them go home hungry.

Chapter 15
Junior Year

Tonndorf Bunker

After being a tour officer for a while, I think every tour officer began to aspire to "the big hit." Something extraordinary, bigger than the norm, something that would become legendary in Mission lore. Not just running columns on the road or covering a big exercise. As exciting as those events were, they were not unusual. In the course of assignment to the Mission, if you just did your share of the tours, you were going to get those. But to be the first to get good photos of a significant new weapons system being deployed into the forward area or evidence of a new type of unit became a desire, if not an objective, of most experienced tour officers. I remember that one of the tour officers got the photography that confirmed the presence of SS-21 missiles in East Germany at the beginning of my tour. I don't think we ever discussed SS-21s in training or BS sessions that someone didn't say, "Oh, yeah, this officer got the first mission pictures of those." I've already mentioned the "Great T-80 Chase" that the French Mission won. And there were others. Putting this in perspective, nothing deployed into East Germany that was not already known through other sources. When we reported a sighting, it was reported at the confidential level—which meant that something that could not be discussed openly because of its classification level could now be discussed by a much wider audience at a much lower classification level. Tour officers from three missions prepared for and hotly pursued the T-80. But only the French had the opportunity.

I guess my biggest opportunity came at a place we referred to from then on as Tonndorf Bunker.

In the 8th Guards Army area, there was a large bunker complex used by the 8GA command group during large exercises. This was located in a forested area north of Dresden and the Koenigsbruek Training Area near the small village of Tonndorf. It was well known to the three allied missions and was routinely checked for activity by almost every Mission team that transited through the area. It was in an open, unsecured forested area and consisted of three large above-ground bunkers—about seventy-five meters long each—and a good-sized parking area in front of the three. There was a caretaker force of guards located in a cabin about two hundred meters from the bunkers. The bunkers always seemed occupied to a small degree because there were nearly always a couple of UAZ-469s (Sov Jeep) parked in bunker parking lots.

The 8GA was significant in that it faced the US Sector in West Germany, particularly at the Fulda Gap (famous to all US Army officers, as that was the point at which we expected Soviet tank and armored forces to pour through if World War III ever really broke out).

Southern East Germany was interesting to me, partly because I had been tapped to do a reconnaissance of routes US units intended to follow in the event they were tasked to launch an attack into East Germany. I felt a little inadequate to the task because all of my time in the infantry had been with light airmobile units, and I would be conducting route reconnaissance for armored units. But I took as a driver, SSG Mike Poindexter, who had served a number of years as a tank driver and sergeant in tank units.

We were provided maps of specific routes and objectives from the East/West German border deep into East Germany almost to the Polish border. It took four days to do it, but we ran every route, providing our assessment of what the route could handle in various weather conditions. We identified choke points and alternative routes. We videotaped and took panoramic photography of routes and key features. We answered particular questions. We identified issues that could not be picked up from a map reconnaissance.

There was not a bit of excitement in this trip—no chases or close calls. Yet it was very satisfying for me personally—an infantry officer—to brief this staff on their plan.

But, again, I digress. Back to the 8GA headquarters bunker complex. This is an area that I visited many times while a tour officer, but never encountered much activity. It was also the location of one of my three detentions. The detention itself was very low key. I was with Ron Blake, and we had been scouting the bunker complex without noting anything of significance. As we drove north out of the area, we discovered that we had two flat tires. One would have been okay because we had a spare. But two crippled us. We limped to an intersection just north of the headquarters bunkers, which, amazingly, had a functioning telephone booth. We parked the G-wagon next to the phone booth and called back to the Potsdam house for rescue. We were a good three or four hours south of Potsdam, so we knew we had a good time to wait. A couple of Sov vehicles went by, so I was not surprised when about a half-hour later a group of Sovs showed up in two trucks (ZIL-131) and a UAZ-469 accompanied by two carloads of East German security guys.

They immediately began positioning the two ZILs in front of and behind the G-wagon—so close that the bumpers were nearly touching our vehicle. Then, they proceeded to wrap cables around the two bumpers. The security guys got out and began photographing everything, so I put my Kodak 110 camera in my pocket and got out of the G-wagon. I looked at the scene and started laughing. The Sov Captain who seemed to be in charge walked over to me with a couple of his soldiers, and I pointed to the tires and asked him where he thought we were going with two flat tires. He did not respond, so I pulled my camera out of my pocket and began photographing the scene to include the East German security guys. I was sure this was going to get a reaction and I was right. I was ignoring them except for the photos; so they went into a huddle with the Sovs and pretty quickly the captain came to me and demanded the film from my camera. I told him that the security guys had documented the scene with their camera and I was only doing the same. I could tell that he didn't really care one way or another; so I pulled my camera out to take more pictures. They pressed him again, and he came back one more time. I told him that I would give him my film if they would give me theirs. They declined, and the East Germans left shortly thereafter. They definitely did not like having their pictures taken.

The rest of the detention was low key. A major arrived from the Dresden Kommandatura finally and drew up an AKT accusing us of having been inside a restricted area (behind Mission restriction signs). I declined to sign. John Eschrich and Hans Tiffany arrived with spare tires. We changed the tires, and the Kommandatura escorted us about ten kilometers out of the area, and we all went our separate ways.

At any rate I had been to this area a good number of times without ever seeing much to report. But late in my second year, I was checking the area (SSG John Johnson was my driver) and I found a new bunker about five hundred meters from the main bunker complex and about the same from the caretaker cabin. It did not look particularly new, but it was not on any of our target folders. It was buried entirely underground and had two entrances about thirty meters apart. There were awnings over the stairs that went down to the bunker doors. The doors were definitely new, and a type that I had seen before in various stages of assembly; so I knew that to open them I only needed to turn one bolt with a wrench. Since it was a low-key day—we were five hundred meters from anyone in the area, and this bunker was not in our target folder—I decided to take a look.

I stuck my Canon SureShot Camera in my pocket and got an adjustable wrench from the tool kit. I was right: one quarter turn on the bolt and the bunker door popped open. I could see immediately that the bunker was actively in use and was set up for a major exercise. It was composed of three sectors all accessible from the door that I had entered. It quickly became apparent that it was the 8GA Air Defense Command and Control Bunker. The first large room was dedicated to managing 8GA air defense assets. There were five field phones set up, each one labeled with the Field Post Number (FPN) of the air defense unit at the other end of the line (FPNs were somewhat like US APOs). The Sovs often used them as shorthand for unit names. The room was divided into two parts: one an operational area (where the field phones were), and then a room for tracking the status of units on a large glass wall that had maps drawn on it; and where, reminiscent of a World War II war room, soldiers behind the glass wall could post and move unit symbols.

I will return to the second room in a moment, but the third room was configured similarly to the first room, except that it was dedicated to the enemy situation—particularly NATO and the US. There were charts on the wall that tracked the status of our spy satellites and various nuclear assets. It had the same glass wall on which NATO assets could be tracked real time. This one had a map painted on it that stretched across the US sector of West Germany.

The center room was the largest of the three and was configured to combine information from the other two. On one wall was a diagram showing the expected configuration and tactics of US forces committed against the 8GA area.

I was pretty excited. This all looked pretty cool to me, and I was photographing it all. In the third room, my batteries started to die, and it was taking the flash longer and longer to recharge. Things were about to go bad anyhow. I had made two mistakes. First, I had not gotten out of the G-wagon with spare batteries; and, more importantly, I had not checked the bunker door for the telltale detent pin that would have told me the door was alarmed. I was thinking about going back to the car for more batteries when I heard John honk the horn.

I immediately knew I was in trouble. Our normal signal that something was wrong was a rev of the engine. I was deep enough into the bunker that I had not heard the engine rev. If John had honked, I knew we were way beyond engine revving trouble and something was really wrong.

I stuffed my Canon SureShot down in my pocket and started up the covered stairway. My plan was simple enough. If guards had come and they had guns, I would just raise my hands and give up. If they didn't, I would make a run for it. They could not see me until I got to the top step because of the awning. Johnny and the G-wagon were waiting right next to the bunker exit. I would have to cover about ten feet to get to the vehicle door.

I hit the top step and glanced out from the awning, looking for the guards, There were two—one was already at the other bunker entrance, the other guard was walking toward me about fifteen feet away. Neither was armed—I sucked air in for the first time in a couple of minutes. I stepped out from under the awning and started walking for the G-wagon. I nodded to the soldier—he was stunned to see me and halted for a moment. Then he came to life and yelled "Stop!"

I started running and John started rolling. I got to the G-wagon door but dropped the wrench I used to open the bunker door as I jumped into the G-wagon. By this time the guard was running behind the G-wagon pounding on the back window with his fists. But it was too late. We were gone.

We returned to Berlin two days later, and I turned in the film to be developed—a whole roll of about thirty shots—to our photo lab and went home to get some sleep. When I got in the next morning, there was an Intel briefing team visiting USMLM from US European Command (EUCOM), and they were already excitedly going through my pictures. They wanted to hear all about it, including how I got into the bunker. So I ran through the whole thing with them.

This was beginning to feel like the "big hit" to me. Later that day, I got a personal phone call from the Commander of the Strategic Air Command's Executive Assistant, passing on thanks for a job well done. However, the EUCOM briefing team returned to EUCOM and briefed the Tonndorf bunker photos a few days later. In their briefing, they embellished the story of how I got into the bunker, including slipping past guards and bypassing cypher locks—none of which was correct, but which raised significant concerns on the part of the deputy commander of EUCOM—a four-star general who got on his plane and flew directly to Berlin. Colonel Lajoie was on leave, so the general met with me and the USMLM Deputy Chief, Air Force Lieutenant Colonel Larry Shofner. We sat quietly while the general chewed us out for being cowboys and taking big chances which threatened a very delicate balance between the US and the Soviet Union. He was particularly incensed about me sneaking passed guards and bypassing the cypher lock. He was on "transmit" and was not looking for any response from us, so after about thirty minutes of very one-sided discussion, he got up and left. For the next few days, I wasn't sure if I was going to get an award or get court-martialed. Finally, it all kind of just balanced out and faded away.

This wasn't quite the end of the story, however. I was told that the air tactics shown on the wall in the big room (the one that showed the tactics that they expected the US to use) were all wrong. But to encourage the Sovs to continue to train against incorrect tactics, USAFE staged a training exercise using the wrong tactics in the 8GA sector so that the Sovs could monitor it and reinforce their misperceptions.

There was one other interesting development for me, personally. A couple of weeks later, I got a phone call from one of our attachés in Moscow. He was a friend of mine and had been at USMLM before he went to Moscow. He did not know anything about Tonndorf Bunker, but said that he had been stopped on the street in Moscow by Stefan Maltsev, one of the officers assigned to the Soviet External Relations Branch (SERB) in Potsdam. The attaché knew Maltsev, and so did I. Maltsev told him to pass a warning on to me that I was being too aggressive and that I needed to back off. He said if I didn't understand that he had my wrench (the one I dropped during the getaway from the bunker). The attaché asked if I knew what Maltsev was referring to and, of course, I did. I told him thanks for the warning. I didn't change anything about my touring style, but I did pay extra attention to security for a while.

But as for the "big hit," this was as close as I got. I suppose being chewed out by a four-star general and getting a special warning from the Sovs delivered in Moscow meant that it was important to someone.

Chapter 16

Perks

In addition to our normal recon missions, we were authorized—no, encouraged—to take "representational" or "cultural" tours into East Germany. These were low-key trips without any intelligence targets assigned—more of "show the flag" trip. We could take our wives and treat it like a weekend outing. With sufficient planning in advance, we could even take friends or visiting relatives into East Germany on site-seeing excursions. Potsdam had several points of interest—Kaiser Wilhelm's Neu Palais (New Palace) and "Sans Souci" the summer palace, as well as the site at which Truman, Stalin, and Churchill negotiated the final capitulation and division of Germany into four sectors plus Berlin.

The Mission Potsdam House was technically the headquarters of USMLM. In earlier years the Mission liaison officers lived in houses on the road leading from the turnoff of Route 2 to the mission house. In the '80s we all lived in very comfortable quarters in West Berlin—expertly maintained by the Berlin Brigade. Because the Potsdam House was the official headquarters of USMLM, it was manned one hundred percent of the time by a US Army Officer or NCO. Manning and managing the house was a serious function and normally an Army lieutenant or captain lived the five week days of the week at the house. On the weekends, however, the House Father, as he was known within the mission, got a break, and the house sitting job was rotated among the Mission staff currently holding credentials. The house was staffed by about six or eight East Germans (routinely debriefed by the staff of the

Soviet External Relations Branch [SERB]). The staff included cleaning personnel, maintenance personnel, and cooks. So, when you were tasked to house sit on a weekend, many of us considered it to be a perk. You could take a book, some VHS movie tapes (remember those?), and spend the entire weekend being waited upon hand and foot by the house staff. In addition, and again with a little planning, you could even take guests for the weekend. The house staff would even prepare special meals—a house specialty while I was there was Peking duck.

For my wife and I, this became part of the Berlin routine. If we had friends or relatives come to visit, we would arrange for private tours of the Kaiser Wilhelm Neu Palais and the Summer Palace and for dinner at the Potsdam house. We were required to use Mission vehicles, so we would use either one of the Mercedes 350 SL sedans or the VW Microbus, depending on the size of our group. Because, from the Soviet's perspective, these little excursions were just like any other tour, we crossed into Potsdam from West Berlin at the Soviet Checkpoint on the Glienicke Bridge—another interesting aspect of the trip for most of our guests.

We also took tourist-like trips to Dresden and Leipzig to visit Meissen Porcelain museums and factories. East German crystal products were every bit as good as West German, and we collected a number of beautiful pieces.

In addition to these official liaison functions, there was a good relationship between USMLM and the British Mission (BRIXMIS) and the French Mission (FMLM), which was reinforced by routine social interactions. Official functions (British Tattoos, Guy Faulks Day, visits by the Royal Family, Officer Dining-Ins) and French functions, such as an elaborate annual costume ball, and reciprocal events by the US, such as our fourth of July picnic and Thanksgiving Day dinners, were all accompanied by routine invitations to the other mission (and often to the Soviets as well). One of the highlights of living in Berlin was that US officers had equal access to the British Officer's Club (superb atmosphere) and the French Officer's Club (excellent French cuisine)—and the US Officer's Club was like US Military Officers' clubs used to be. We took advantage of other perks as well; my wife was a member of the British Riding Club, which was as formal as you might expect. She loved it.

Being in Berlin itself was a unique experience. Completely surrounded by walls, routine stories of attempted escapes, and reasonably easy access to cultural activities, such as museums, orchestras, and the Soviet War Memorial in

East Berlin via Checkpoint Charlie. The virtual isolation of Berlin emphasized by the wall and the duty train from Helmstedt to Berlin and the strict vehicle traffic adherence to the autobahn route from Check Point Alpha to Bravo all created a special atmosphere in Berlin that was unique to the time and place.

The Berlin zoo and the underground transport system (that in places crossed under East Berlin), Kaufhaus Des Westin, the Gedaktnes Kirche, Brandenburg Gate, Hitler's Bunker, the Reichstag building, the Tier Park, the Kurfurstendam (or KuDamm as the soldiers called it)—all special to Cold War Berlin gave Berlin an atmosphere unlike that of any other city in which I have lived or visited. Living at the true cutting edge of two conflicting cultures gave everyone a special sense of being alive and appreciation of the harshness and reality of the struggle between the East and West.

Another part of just living in Berlin that had a unique character was Christmas. My wife and I attended the Post Chapel and sang in the Chapel Choir. Each year during the month of December, there was a special program called the "Allied Choir Christmas Program" that was performed in the Kaiser Wilhelm Gedaktnes Kirche on the Kurfurstendam in the center of Berlin. The beautiful, old church had been destroyed during World War II. The Germans had never rebuilt it, but left only the bombed-out main steeple standing as a reminder of the devastation of war. Next to the old steeple they had built a very modernistic amphitheater where various services were held. The Allied Choir was composed of choirs from the German, American, British, and French communities in Berlin. The American community was represented by the Berlin Brigade Chapel Choir. Each choir had about twenty to thirty members and joined in the singing of several carols jointly; and then, individually, they would sing two or three traditional national carols. Between carols the Christmas story was read in three languages and prayers offered. The program was presented over three evenings and rebroadcast over the radio on Christmas Eve.

East Germany was a sad place at Christmas time—especially when compared with West Germany. None of the beautiful white lights and Christmas trees found in the store windows; and the most visible Christmas (or New Year) celebration was a German Schwibiggen (carved wooden arch normally placed in the house window). Little else to be seen.

I discovered a small bacherai in the town of Luebben, which had the best Christmas Stoellen that I have ever had. I made a trip there during the first week of December to buy about twenty of them. During my last year, the Sovs redrew the PRA maps, and my bacherai fell into the restricted area (one side of the street was in, the other out). PRA's be damned. I got my Christmas Stoellen.

My wife worked as a Budget Analyst for the Berlin Military Community, and she had a number of German and British friends. They routinely passed through Check Point Charlie into East Berlin to attend cultural events such as operas and symphonies or to shop. The Soviet Cemetery, with its bowed weeping willows, was always a moving sight to visit. There wasn't that much to buy, but some things were exquisite, such as crystal. There were several good restaurants in East Germany where you could feed a group of twenty for about a quarter of what it would cost in West Germany.

When relatives or friends came to visit us in Berlin, we usually arranged to get them temporary passes, and we would have lunch or dinner at the Potsdam House and a private tour of Kaiser Wilhelm's Neu Palais (new palace) and/or Sans Souci (the summer palace). Walking tours in the center of Potsdam could also be very picturesque. We sometimes visited the building in which Truman, Stalin, and Churchill signed the agreements that ended World War II and divided Germany. And, of course, the trip to the Potsdam House was a treat all by itself.

Being in Berlin itself was a unique experience. Completely surrounded by walls, routine stories of attempted escapes and reasonably easy access to cultural activities such as museums, orchestras, and the Soviet War Memorial in East Berlin via Checkpoint Charlie. The virtual isolation of Berlin emphasized by the wall and the duty train from Helmstedt to Berlin and the strict vehicle traffic adherence to the autobahn route from Check Point Alpha to Bravo all created a special atmosphere in Berlin that was unique to the time and place.

Another perk, we had access occasionally to a helicopter tour of the city that was spectacular. Then, there were monuments and historical sites like the Tiergarten, the Reichstag, the Brandenburg Gate, Hitler's bunker, the Check Point Charlie Museum, and the Soviet War Memorial. The Berlin Zoo was a special treat always.

Shopping and restaurants along the Kurfurstendamm, or Kudamm, as the troops called it, was excellent. My wife and I frequented a Currywurst Stand at the very end of the Kurfurstendamm, which was famous locally for being the original source for Currywurst.

My wife was a member of the British Riding Club in the British sector—every bit as formal as you might imagine from a British Club; she loved it. One year while we were there, the Germans decided to host an international jumping event. There were four Americans in the British club, so they asked them to form a team so they would have four countries represented. The Americans won. They didn't do it again the next year.

My hobby is shooting, and I kept the Berlin Brigade Rod & Gun Club solvent, as well as making frequent use of Rose Range.

Probably the best perk we had was living in a duplex provided by the Berlin Brigade in a mixed German-American neighborhood about a half a mile from the USMLM Operational Headquarters in Berlin. Our place was a duplex by virtue of the fact that our carport joined the duplex next door. We had a big yard with forty trees in it. The first year we were there, I picked up the leaves by myself (well, Dru helped). I picked up 110 yard bags full of leaves. Once was enough. The next three years I left it to a handyman that worked our neighborhood. It was a typical military community; about half of the tour officers lived nearby, which made for a very active social life.

Another perk that I failed to take advantage of, but others did, and that was selective shopping in East Germany. Down around the town of Suhl were master gunmakers. German gunmakers from this region were known for producing "drillings"—multi-barreled rifle/shotgun combinations; usually three barrel combinations, such as 7mm rifle, 20-gauge shotgun, and .22 rim fire, and sometimes a fourth barrel. If made in West Germany they were quite expensive, but I could have bought one using East German marks. The factory in Suhl was outside of any Permanent Restricted Area, so I had easy access. I just never got around to it. It was my biggest failure while at the mission. The shopping was not so great overall, but select things such as antiques, crystal, porcelain, and stamps (for collectors) were all good buys if you took time to look.

I have already mentioned the British and French Officers Clubs, but there were other perks that arose from living in the divided city, such as British dining-ins, tattoos, a formal visit by Prince Charles, Guy Faulkes Day—to which I was invited on several occasions by Majors Jeremy York and Simon Cleveland, both Chiefs of Ground Operations in BRIXMIS. The French invited us to a number of social events, including an elaborate all-night costume ball.

I am not sure that I would call it a perk because it was an official function, but each year on the fourth of July we would host a picnic and invite the other missions and the staff at SERB. It was work, but I enjoyed it just the same. It traditionally included a volleyball game between the US and Sovs. The Sov delegation always included four or five officers we had never seen before but were all about six foot six and great volleyball players who would pound us into the ground. The Sovs don't like losing to Americans—even in backyard volleyball. It was fun because we (tour officers and NCOs) could engage in somewhat normal conversations and interact socially with the SERB staff. Normally my only direct interaction with SERB was in some kind of a confrontation.

Official functions fell into the same category. Hosted either by USMLM at Potsdam House or the Sovs at their Officers Club in Potsdam, these events could be quite enjoyable and interesting. I remember one reception at the Sov Officers Club, where I was assigned to stick close to a US Brigadier General from USAREUR to facilitate his conversation with Russian officers. While he engaged with a Soviet general, I noticed the Soviet general was taking drinks from the back of the tray when offered by a Soviet soldier/server. I did the same at the next opportunity, only to discover that the drinks at the front of the tray were Vodka while those at the back were water. Another lesson learned.

I am a Christmas person. Ask my family or any of my friends and they will tell you that Christmas is a big deal to me. I love everything about it. I love the food, I love the music, I love the crowds, the shopping, the cards. I start planning things in mid-November and begin doing Christmassy things after dinner on Thanksgiving Day. Just because we were living behind the iron curtain surrounded by atheistic Sovs, I was not going to be deterred. Actually, I felt sorry for the East Germans. West Germans are so festive at Christmas time and the East Germans were so repressed. It was sad to me as I traveled throughout East Germany that many cottages or apartments would have in a window facing the street a wooden carving in the form of an arch with eight or nine candles (or sometimes electric lights) in an arch over the top. But the figures were not Christian, but usually workers of the proletariat with a hammer and cycle somewhere as a prominent part of the display. I guess the workers were making toys and that was supposed to give it a Christmas theme. Most houses or apartments displayed one of these during December. Occasionally I would also see a small Christmas tree through a window. As opposed to West Germany, where churches had Christmas concerts and music, there was nothing in East Germany.

I have mentioned before that we always had tours operating in East Germany twenty-four-seven, and Christmas was no exception. Since I had no kids, I wound up pulling the local on Christmas Eve two out of the four years that I was at the mission. John Eschrich's family liked pulling Potsdam House Duty on Christmas Eve, and I think he volunteered for that duty every year that we were there. John and his family were very good friends to Dru and me, so on Christmas Eve, Dru would drive to Glienecke Bridge and park her car, and I would pick her up on the bridge; and we would join Eschrichs for Christmas Eve dinner, which would have been prepared by the East German staff before they went home on Christmas Eve.

I suspect the Soviets did it intentionally because it was Christmas Eve in the West; but both times that I pulled the local on Christmas Eve, it seemed to me like every garrison around Berlin staged a crash out exercise around 6 p.m., drove around for about an hour, and then went back into their garrisons around 7:30 p.m. Just enough to remind us that they didn't care about Christmas. Both years I chased the various columns until dinner time, went to the bridge to pick up Dru, and went back to the Potsdam House for dinner. By the time that I got back to the house, things had calmed down again, and we had an enjoyable dinner with John and Vonda and their kids.

Well, I was a member of the chapel choir. I don't read music. I don't play an instrument. My mother was a choir director for as long as I can remember, and I always sang in her choirs. Since I don't read music and I have virtually no sense of rhythm, I watch the director very closely. Directors love anyone that pays attention to them, so they always like me. I do have a pretty good ear and, in those days, could carry a tune pretty well. Not solo quality but I did alright in a crowd. Well, the chiefs of the allied missions decided that we would have a joint Christmas Party and each mission would sing several carols. Being the only member of USMLM with known associations with choirs, I was designated to organize USMLM's "choir." I will confess to a decided lack of enthusiasm but quickly realized there was no gracious way out, so I came up with a plan. Since the US was a melting pot of culture, I came up with several songs that pretty much everyone knew but that were French and British in origin, as well as a couple from American pop culture. Supported by the Chief of Ground (LTC Govan) to get everyone to come to at least one practice, and the assistance of his wife, Jane, on the piano, it went off pretty well. And I have to admit, I did enjoy the party.

There was one other perk that US Officers had while serving in Berlin which I particularly enjoyed at Christmas, and that was the officers' clubs. The US Club was the way that I remembered them from years before, when I was a boy living in Wiesbaden with my father, who was a lieutenant colonel in the Air Force, and to a lesser degree when I first joined the Army. Great atmosphere and excellent food. The US Berlin Officers Club was a pleasure to be a member. But an additional perk was that we had access to the French and British officers clubs. The French Club did not have as great an atmosphere but had the great French cuisine you would expect from a French club. But my real favorite was the British Officers Club. It had excellent food (my favorite desert was a flaming baked Alaska), but the atmosphere was what made it exceptional. It had a very clubby aura like a British Regimental Mess. My wife and I loved to take guests there, especially around the holidays when it was decorated for Christmas.

All of this is to say that living in Berlin was very pleasant when you were not in East Germany being chased, ambushed, or shot at.

Chapter 17
Junior Year

Vehicles

One of the things that I learned pretty quickly was how fast certain vehicles were and how much of a threat they were when you encountered them in a hostile environment. In my mind, a hostile environment could be defined as any place that you encountered someone who did not want you to be where you were.

Now this is just my opinion, but the wheeled vehicles most likely to react to our presence and come after us were the UAZ-469 (Sovs called them WAZEEKs) or GAZ-66 light trucks. Both were two axles and four wheel drive. With a good driver, they were nearly as fast as our G-Wagons and just as mobile. When they decided to seriously pursue us, it was going to be a long afternoon. I remember being with Steve Eairheart, running south out of Potsdam on Route 2, one day, and running into a traffic jam. As we watched, we could see a roiling dust cloud, where vehicles on our side of the road had stopped. The dust was so dense that we could not see clearly what was going on, so we rolled up the left side of the road to get a better view. As we got closer, we could see that it was an armored unit of some size crossing the highway on an east/west tac trail. There was so much dust that we could not see what was on the other side of the road. Initially we could see tanks in the dust and then BMPs (tracked armored personnel carriers). They were passing at a rate of about one every five or six seconds. We started counting and then shot across the tac trail between two BMPs. From the opposite side we could see the column of vehicles more clearly, so we picked a spot in the woods across a plowed field that gave us a good panorama of the moving column. Out came the camera and binoculars, and we were getting it all.

Suddenly Steve sits up sharply and begins to crank up the G-wagon and yells, "We've got to go!" I glanced back, and there was a UAZ-469 about one hundred meters back and coming fast. Steve got us rolling, and we made a run for the paved road—about five hundred meters away. We made the road and turned away from the tac trail on the paved road. The UAZ, still about one hundred meters back, stayed right with us. As we ran south on Route 2, we passed another UAZ headed north. Something about it caught my attention, and, as I watched, it did a U-turn behind us and joined the pursuing UAZ. They stayed with us for about five kilometers, at which point they dropped off. We continued another kilometer; then turned into the woods and ran back woods trails to get back to the column. More cautiously now we monitored the tac trail for about an hour until they found us and we had to jump and run again. This process repeated itself with minor variations for the next four or five hours. The point being that we really couldn't outrun them. They stayed with us until they felt that we had cleared the area and then continued to patrol for us near the tac trail where they knew we wanted to be.

GAZ-66s were two-axled light trucks—about as fast as the UAZ but big enough to do some damage if they rammed us. If the Kommandatura arrived in force, it was almost always in a GAZ.

Several other trucks we had to watch out for—not because they were fast, but because they were frequently used in ambushes to block exit routes, primarily the ZIL-131 and the URAL-375. These were the workhorses of the Soviet Military and equivalent to the US Military two-and-a-half ton truck. These trucks could get up some speed, but they could not turn quickly or easily; so we could easily out maneuver them if in an open area that allowed for maneuvering. But if one of them was after you, as long as you had access to a paved road somewhere, you could always get away. That is not to say you didn't need to worry about them. I mentioned earlier the attempted ambush at the northern edge of the Koenigsbruek Training Area. The truck they tried to close the trap for us with was a ZIL-131. They all had large winches mounted in the front bumper, and all I remember seeing, as that truck lurched forward trying to block or ram us, was that monstrous winch which nearly filled the window on the driver's side as we shot by. Another two seconds delay and that winch would have been in the back seat. All trucks could be dangerous. Both the Sovs and the East Germans used a non-tactical two-and-a-half ton truck called a ZIL-130, which was used for lighter duty support. Not as agile as a GAZ-66 or as lumbering as a ZIL-131, it was one of these that swerved from an East German column and rammed a French Mission vehicle, killing the driver, Marriotti, and putting the warrant officer passenger in the hospital and rehab for over a year during my second year at the Mission. And if you will remember my story about being chased from an East German SA-5 site with Major Skip Bohn, those were East German ZIL-555 dump trucks that tried to ram us.

Armored vehicles were another category entirely. Our G-wagons were faster than any of the armored personnel carriers, but cross-country or down a rugged road they had the advantage. I don't ever remember a tank breaking out of a moving column to chase a Mission vehicle. It may have happened, but I never saw it. On the other hand, I saw an East German Trabant Sedan that had been run over by a T-64 tank, where a tac trail intersected a two-lane paved road, and the back half of the Trabant was as flat at a pancake. So, I maintained a steady respect for tanks.

Armored personnel carriers tracked and wheeled were a different story. If you were monitoring a column movement and were seen by personnel from vehicles in the column, it was almost certain that at some point vehicles would either break out of the column or be dispatched to chase us off. The big-wheeled armored personnel carriers (BTR-60, BTR-70) were big, eight-wheeled vehicles and took time and space to turn. Tracked vehicles (BMP-1, BMP-2) were capable of doing pivot turns and could turn on a dime in a small space. Steve Eairheart and I were watching a BMP-equipped motorized rifle unit move down a tac trail. We were watching from about seventy-five meters down a very narrow firebreak. I thought we were perfectly safe, unless some-one came from behind us; and the column was passing so quickly I thought it was unlikely that they even noticed that we were there. All of a sudden a BMP on the tac trail did a pivot turn right onto our firebreak and came crashing down the trail. We were able to get away, but the BMP was close before we got up the momentum to break contact.

The recon/scout vehicles (BRDM-1, BRDM-2) were two-axled and quite fast, and they were frequently posted around a training area, specifically to chase off Mission vehicles. My rule was that we paid close attention to the recon vehicles, as they were the most likely to react if they saw us.

Much bigger vehicles could be a threat also. Pontoon Bridge units were mounted on huge KRAZ-255B trucks, nineteen to the set, and nearly always led by a UAZ-469 with a radio. Running a column of bridge sections head on a two-lane highway could be very exciting. And I have already mentioned being with Paul Nelson on my first training tour and being chased by a GTS Ferry, which is a tracked vehicle large enough to carry a tank inside.

So, I learned to respect the danger represented by all types of Sov vehicles—some more than others.

Chapter 18
Senior Year Begins

My third year as a tour officer began somewhat inauspiciously. I received orders from infantry branch assigning me to duty as Assistant Professor of Military Science at Kansas State University. That didn't sound too bad to me. Kansas had good hunting, was just north of Oklahoma—where the rest of my family lived—was part of the Big Eight Conference, which meant good college football, and Kansas also had a pro football team. But I could see two problems. First, I was on a three-year utilization tour, which was payback for the Army for all of the time that I had spent in school. Second, with all of the schooling and utilization tour, I would have been away from the infantry for seven years. That was nearly a killer of my infantry career already. If I got another tour away from the infantry, there would be no recovery.

So, I called infantry branch and ran through this with them. They agreed with point one and annotated my records to indicate another year at the Mission. Then, I asked about point two, and the assignments officer was quite blunt. He said he had a number of positions like this that required master's degrees, and he asked, "Who in the infantry has master's degrees? It's all of you foreign area officers." I could see the handwriting on the wall. He had already written me off as an infantry officer. This was not a shock to me—it merely confirmed what I suspected would happen. I knew the FAO assignments officer had more positions to fill than he had officers, so at that moment I became committed to the FAO program and never looked back. I was only disappointed by this decision once in the rest of my career.

My senior year was characterized by several key points. One, I knew what I was doing. I never stopped studying Soviet order of battle and equipment; I never stopped practicing sneaking around installations and blowing off security; and I never stopped preparing properly for tours or finishing them off with reporting. But I was very comfortable with it. Two, I was bored. Because I knew the Sov training cycle, I knew within a couple of hours of getting into an area whether we were going to have an exciting tour or not. It made me nervous because I knew that when people got bored they also got lax, and that is when people made mistakes. So, I forced myself to be extra cautious in preparations and execution of missions. Third, as a senior tour officer, there were perks. This is when I discovered that I really had learned some things by virtue of seeing them myself that others did not know.

I have mentioned "detentions" off and on here, but, to summarize, I was caught four times—one of which I talked my way out of. First, I was caught with Ron Blake just north of the 8GA command bunker area when we managed to get two flat tires and the Sovs blocked our crippled vehicle in. Second, I got caught with John Johnson at the north Elbe river-crossing site when a Soviet Lieutenant smashed our windshield with a shovel.

My third detention was with Dave Boone in the northern edge of the Koenigsbruek training area. Most of the Koenigsbruek training area was located in a PRA, but a portion of the north edge was arguably outside; so, we were checking that area for T-80 tanks, which were being deployed to the 11th Guards Tank Division. We had been in the area for about an hour and had been seen by several soldiers in the area on foot. I figured we had about outstayed our welcome, as the soldiers had enough time to get back to their units and report having seen us. We headed for our planned exit route, only to discover that it was blocked by a large and apparently deep water obstacle that stretched completely across the trail. Dave gave it a shot, but we bogged down exactly in the middle of it. I got out and got the winch cable and waded to the other side of the puddle and wrapped the cable around a tree. As I did so, two UAZ-469s stopped on the other side of the puddle behind the G-wagon. After a minute, the second one turned around and headed back down the trail. We were stuck pretty good; the winch was struggling to pull us out. I could hear armored vehicles cranking up in the distance, and pretty quickly two BMP-1 came into sight. I could see that their intention was to run quickly through the puddle and get in front of us, so I waved for them to stop and pointed at our winch cable. They stopped, and I untied our winch cable and moved out of the way. At which point the lead BMP came on across the puddle and stopped on the dry ground beside me. A warrant officer climbed out of the BMP turret and climbed down beside me. I was still holding the winch cable, so I just handed it to him. He quickly wrapped it around a tie down point on the back of the BMP, and they yanked the G-wagon out of the mud puddle. I'm not sure what Dave was thinking, but as he cleared the puddle I reached up and popped the cable loose from the BMP. Dave gunned the engine trying to get in front of the BMP, at which point everyone got excited. The BMP that had just yanked us out of the puddle did an immediate pivot turn and hit the side of the G-Wagon—nearly running over both the warrant officer and me. I dove out of the way and yelled for Dave to stop—which he did. I was trying to get everyone to calm down; there was a lot of yelling going on between the Sovs, ultimately resulting in the two BMPs being cabled to our front and rear bumpers. At about this moment, two more UAZ-469s rolled up loaded with officers from the unit. I could see from their uniform insignia that they were from a motorized rifle unit, and in a few minutes one of the officers introduced himself as the regimental commander. We began a discussion of whether I was allowed to be in this location. I showed them my PRA map and told them I had been here many times. I pointed to a location on the map and said that is where we were standing—clearly outside of the PRA. The commander took my map and he and several of his officers began comparing with their maps. I could hear them arguing, some agreeing with my point, others arguing that I was in the training area—I must be in the PRA. Ultimately it didn't make any difference. Their responsibility was to detain us or chase us off. Now that they had detained us, they did not have the authority to release us. Once detained the incident had to be investigated and documented by the Kommandatura.

A major from the Dresden Kommandatura's office finally arrived. He asked a bunch of questions of the unit personnel and spent another half-hour writing up the AKT. Then he and I, and the regimental commander, got into one of their UAZ-469s, and he asked for my credentials. I pulled out my wallet and gave him my pass and threw my wallet on the dashboard.

I don't have any children, but I have five nephews and a niece, and I carried their pictures in my wallet. My wallet fell open (intentionally) to the photos of my nephews and niece. I could see both officers glancing at them, and within a minute they both had their wallets out and were showing me pictures of their kids. From that point on we were all just soldiers a long way from home and wanting a good life for the kids. We chatted about life in general for about thirty minutes. They presented the AKT, which I congenially and respectfully refused to sign. They returned my PRA map and escorted Dave and me to the north end of the training area, at which point we all shook hands and departed to our own destinations. All in all, I considered it a very pleasant several hours.

I was caught one other time that could have been considered a detention if I had not talked our way out of it.

Near the end of my tour, the Sovs issued a new PRA map (they did this two or three times while I was at the Mission), and, of course, we were interested in exploring areas that had been in PRAs previously but were no longer protected. One area that was open under the new map was a series of rail sidings north of Dallgow-Doeberitz and routinely used by the 35th MRD. I was sure that it was going to become a routine target for the local and we would need a target folder. By the map, there was one way in and one way out; and the way in was about a kilometer long before you got to the loading ramp. If that was correct, it was going to be pretty dicey covering this rail siding—whether or not it was in a PRA. Jesse Schatz was driving, and we just drove straight in. On top of being one way in and out, it was pretty close quarters with rails on both sides of the road. On the opposite side of the rails on our right was another road running parallel to the one we were on.

Within a few minutes, we had drawn attention and two UAZ-469s were right behind us obviously with intentions of blocking us in.

Jesse asked me, "Do you want me to jump the tracks?"

I had been with Jesse before when we had "jumped the tracks" and, not only was it really rough, it scared the dickens out of me. If you didn't make it on the first try, rocking your way out of it was nerve-wracking. My grandfather had died of injuries incurred in a car/train accident, and I did not want to be the second Wyckoff to do so. Besides, this was no longer a restricted area, and we had a right to be there.

So I said, "No, just pull over."

As expected, one vehicle pulled up right behind us and the other pulled in front to block our escape. I got out of the G-Wagon and a major got out of the lead vehicle. From his uniform insignia, I could see that he was a motorized rifle officer, probably from one of the local regiments. I asked him why he had blocked us in. He accused us of violating a restricted area. I pulled out my newly issued PRA map and showed him that this was no longer in a restricted area. He seemed genuinely confused, but—as I have mentioned before—having stopped us, he did not have the authority to release us. We waited for about thirty minutes until an officer from the Potsdam Kommandatura arrived to take charge from the Soviet side and investigate the situation. Quickly confirming that the area was, in fact, no longer inside of a PRA and that there was no military activity underway that we should be blocked from, he simply let us go. No AKT, no escort from the area.

I guess I should say that I have never hated Russians or Soviets, even though, as the Sovs put it, they were the "glavnii protivniks"—the main enemy. I knew that they were armed with nuclear weapons that were aimed at us, that they had scared us by putting satellites and a man in space before us. I was in high school during the Cuban Missile Crisis. I knew they did whatever they could to beat us wherever they came in contact with Americans. As an infantry officer, post-Vietnam, we trained to fight against the Soviet military. They had the biggest bombs, the biggest tanks, they were ten feet tall, lean and mean. One of the reasons that I became a Soviet foreign area officer was that I wanted to see these guys for myself. I wanted to know who they were and what they were all about. It was my good fortune that Nick Nicholson and I became such good friends because he had the same attitude—a total fascination with the nature of the "main enemy" but not a lot of personal animosity.

Nick and I became friends at the Naval Postgraduate School and Defense Language Institute in Monterey while getting our master's degrees in National Security Affairs; and continued our friendship at the US Army Russian Institute (USARI), where we shared an office and lived across the hall from each other in the community housing area. Our families became friends, and we shared many holiday celebrations together. It was only natural that we would become traveling partners during USARI class trips into Eastern Europe and the Soviet Union. We both learned quickly that, on our class trips, we were not interested in tourist sites—we wanted to meet the enemy. So, everywhere we went, when we had free time, we got on a bus and went to the end of the line, just to see if we could meet and chat with some normal people. The institute had a two-man rule in effect, so, as long as there were two of us together, no one objected to our approach.

The first thing that Nick and I discovered (that remained consistent through the rest of my career dealing with Soviets and Russians) was that ten feet tall or not, they were not liked at all by their supposed allies; but they did not seem aware of this, We talked to lots of people, but our first hurdle outside of Russia was that we spoke English and Russian. While traveling in the countries of the Warsaw Pact, if we could not find someone to chat with in English, even though we were certain that there were people around us that understood Russian, no one would talk to us until we managed to explain that we were lost Americans and only spoke English and Russian. Then sometimes people would speak to us.

Some funny things happened to us doing this. In Warsaw we got lost. We went far enough out that we got off the edge of our map, and, when we got ready to go back to the hotel, we could not find the bus stop we needed. There was a lady selling ice cream from the window of her apartment on a street corner, so, looking as pitiful as we could, we asked her if she spoke English and if she could help us.

She looked at us with a funny expression on her face and said in near perfect English, "Of course I speak English. My sister lives in Chicago, and I go there three months every summer."

So, we bought ice cream bars, and she showed us how to get back to the hotel.

We did the same thing in Russia. We would talk to anyone. One afternoon we spent about two hours talking to some cleaning ladies. It was a surprise to both of us that these ladies, probably in their late forties or early fifties, were die-hard communists. They thought the Soviet system was working pretty well, and they had nothing good to say about the US government. It was a real education for me. I began to discover a pattern that remained steady until the Soviet Union collapsed and was reinforced many times in many conversations subsequently. Most Soviet citizens never traveled outside of their country. They had a view of the US that was based in the 1930's because that is what they were told and they had nothing to compare that view against. Why should they not believe what they were being told? Those who did travel became cynics.

I could give a hundred examples of this. We went to see the American movie *Three Days of the Condor*, starring Robert Redford in Moscow. It was well dubbed in Russian, and after a couple of minutes you didn't even think about the Russian anymore. After a few minutes I noticed the crowd murmuring and whispering at odd moments, so I started listening to what they were saying. They were not paying much attention to the plot. What they were talking about was what they could see of American lifestyle—the cars on the street, clothes in the stores, the apartments that people lived in.

One more quick example: Later in life I was leading an arms control inspection team in southern Ukraine under the provisions of the Intermediate Nuclear Forces (INF) Reduction Treaty. The leader of the Soviet escort team was an Air Force Lieutenant Colonel, Valery Yatsenko. The inspection was going well, and late in the day we sat down and began talking. The subject was the US participation in WWII. Russians are taught that the reason that the US and Great Britain did not conduct the Normandy invasion until 1944 was to allow the Germans to defeat the Russian army so that, once we invaded and defeated the Germans, we could then push on into Russia and replace the Soviet state with something more to our liking. This conversation occurred in the summer that the Soviets finally decided, publicly, that the history books in their high schools were so full of inaccuracies and misstatements that they pulled them out of the schools and discarded them. I quickly discovered that what LTC Yatsenko was doing was bouncing what he thought he knew about WWII off of my knowledge. When my answers started sounding more credible than his, I could see his confidence in what he had been told his whole life; I could hear bitterness and cynicism in his voice concerning lies he had been told and believed, since he was a military officer and Soviet patriot.

This then was the picture that began to form in my mind about most Soviet citizens. Most were patriots and loved their country. Whatever its flaws, it had replaced a feudal system with a system that educated its population, provided basic employment for everyone, provided a living space for everyone that was relatively free from street crime. Those that had more information about the Western world and the abuses of power within the Soviet system became cynics. My personal opinion is that the reason that the Soviet Union collapsed so easily was that the number of cynics outnumbered the believers so badly at the end that, when it began to fall, there were not enough believers left to defend it.

Russians are a difficult people to understand anyhow. You had to give them credit. They took a country that was around ninety-five percent illiterate in 1917, and in seventy years they had achieved ninety-five percent literacy. On the other hand, in the same period between the Germans and their own purges, they lost somewhere between forty to sixty million people. Go figure. What a contrast of good and evil.

So, how could you hate people who lived in a world of falsehoods? No one wants to believe that their government is so false that you can't even believe what they publish in their high school text books. I just learned to accept them as they were. I couldn't hate a man that simply believed what his government told him. I could recognize the falseness of the government and train to fight them, but I couldn't hate them.

Chapter 19
Senior Year

Shared Danger

The hot pursuits and ambushes were not just a threat to us. The Sovs took chances themselves when they were chasing us. I have mentioned the ambush at Rohrbeck rail siding, during which a Sov Lieutenant was run over. And I have talked about the Soviet training cycle beginning with drivers training. My guess is that the majority of Sov soldiers had never driven before drivers' training in the military; certainly most of them had never driven a large vehicle like a ZIL-131, URAL-375, or an eight-wheeled armored personnel carrier like a BTR-60 or BTR-70. In the first days of drivers' training, you could see it in their faces. I called it the "white knuckle" period. Most of the drivers were holding on to the steering wheel so tight that there knuckles turned white, and they were so focused on controlling their vehicles that they were not paying attention to anything else. But most of them were typical teenage kids. Behind the wheel for a month and they all thought they were experts. As long as they were in a column in which the speed and turns were controlled by a lead vehicle they did okay. But by themselves they could easily misjudge their ability.

During one of my last tours at the Mission, I was with Gary Lawrence. It was early in the morning on a gray, overcast day. We were in Area A, headed north toward Ludwigslust. The route I had chosen had us transiting near the Redlin-Treptowsee Tank Range. The range was not on our target list—we were merely transiting. As we drove past the firing line (tanks on the range but not firing), I saw a BTR-70 about five hundred meters away on a side road. It was quite a ways off, and we did not even slow down as we went past the tank range. Nevertheless, I saw it start up as we drove through the area. I figured it was there for security, and probably the crew had been told to chase off any Mission vehicles that they saw. So, when I saw the smoke from the exhaust, I told Gary to get on it.

Well they drove from their side rode and got onto the main road, still about five hundred meters behind us. I wasn't worried because, although BTR-70s were fast, they were big and lumbering and not very maneuverable.

We sped up to a little over one hundred KPH, maintaining our distance in front of the BTR. Just north of the tank range was the small village of Jaennersdorf, and in the middle of the town the main road took a hard left turn. At the turn was a large tree at least two feet in diameter (maybe even one full meter) and then a row of farm buildings. We were still moving fast toward the corner, so Gary braked hard, and we went around the corner on two wheels. I noticed there were two farmers on tractors in a courtyard off to the right. The BTR-70 was still coming fast—too fast, I thought.

The road continued to the left for about 150 meters and then jogged back to the right to continue in its original direction. We were about to make the second turn when the BTR came into view—still at full speed. I don't think I will ever forget what happened next for as long as I live.

The BTR-70 is amphibious and has a pointed boat-shaped prow on the front end about one and a half meters high. As I was watching in the rear-view mirror, the BTR-70 hit the large tree at the turn full on. It snapped the tree off with the prow of the vehicle like it was a pencil. It broke the tree at the one-and-a-half meter level, and, as the vehicle's momentum carried it forward, the tree stump launched the BTR fully into the air. My last view of it as we made our turn was of the vehicle with all eight wheels in the air and the severed tree falling directly onto the vehicle commander (who was standing in an open hatch).

I was sick to think of what had happened to the vehicle commander. I was sure that he was dead or badly injured—not to mention the driver and anyone else inside. It was truly a shame, especially since we were only transiting through the area.

It wasn't the only time that Soviet soldiers were at risk. Every close call had two sides to it, and when it came to vehicles I figured that the Sovs often put themselves at as great a risk as us. Not a great comfort, but I considered it my responsibility to avoid putting Soviet soldiers at risk, as well as myself. Considering their safety, as well as ours, was part of the equation of deciding when it was time to stop running and accept a detention.

At Jaennersdorf, in hindsight, I felt bad that someone had been hurt unnecessarily, but other than just pulling over on the side of the road, I don't know what we could have done to have prevented it. Since we were only transiting, I never really even gave a thought to stopping to allow them to detain us.

One other situation that bothered me personally was Soviet hazing. There were lots of articles about brutal hazing by senior troops against newly arriving troops. I guess their conscription service fostered the hazing, but we saw evidence of it. Soviet officers apparently did not feel the same concern that American officers were taught to have, and it showed up in a number of ways. We would often encounter one or two soldiers left in a bivouac site to man a bunker—apparently for several days—often with little food and water. They were glad when we drifted through the biv site, and I carried plenty of extra sandwiches and cigarettes and sodas to give to them. They really didn't often tell us much—if you got the town they were from and what kind of unit they were from you were doing well. But what surprised me most was that they frequently had no idea when they were going to be picked up or replaced. This was also true of the traffic regulators placed on the roads by recon units to direct the movement of following vehicle columns. These guys were put out in the worst of weather, usually only knowing the direction they were to direct the column. In cold weather they were provided heavy overcoats and boots; but when standing on a corner at 0200 in the morning at subzero temperatures that just wasn't enough. But back to the hazing. The worst I ever saw was a traffic regulator on a corner by himself on a sub-zero day around Thanksgiving. Jim McDowell was driving, and I was trying to figure out where the column was coming from; so we pulled up, and I asked the soldier when they were coming and from where. I didn't get much of an answer because his face looked like he had been beaten with a baseball bat. It looked like his nose was broken and probably his jaw too. He could barely move his jaw, but he pointed the direction that the column was coming from. I gave him a bag with six sandwiches, four sodas, and four packs of cigarettes, and he gave me the closest thing to a smile that he could manage. Jim and I took off looking for a place to hide and watch the column movement. I felt so bad for the soldier we went back later with more sandwiches and sodas. I wasn't sure that he could eat a sandwich with his face all banged up, but he had already eaten the others that I gave him and gladly accepted more.

We saw enough of this kind of thing to convince me it was a real problem and not something simply being hyped by the press.

Chapter 20

Just for Fun

Not everything was deadly serious. It was like any other job in that there were times when people would not take life so seriously.

I remember one summer night when I was with Steve Eairhardt and we were targeted to check an installation near Magdeburg. The task would take us close to the installation walls; so we decided we needed two teams, one of which would provide extra security. The second team was Todd Milton and Randy Everett.

Before I go any further, let me say something special about Randy Everett. Randy had two tours at the Mission with more than five hundred tours and never got caught. When you toured with him, you quickly learned why—Randy never slept. He was always on security. I couldn't sleep because I would look over and there was Randy, head on a swivel constantly watching in 360 degrees. I was with him on several occasions that we backed into a target area so that we would be ready to run on a seconds notice.

At any rate, Steve and I were supposed to link up with Todd and Randy in a small clump of trees southwest of the installation at 0200. We got there about 0130, and it was hot so we had the windows rolled down. I was about half asleep when Todd, who, unbeknownst to us, was already there, crawled up next to our G-wagon. For such occasions, Todd carried with him a horrible monster mask, which he had on when he leaped to his feet next to my window and grabbed me. I nearly had a heart attack.

Another time I was returning from a tour with Smitty when Soviet Foxbats (twin-tailed fighter aircraft) began flying down the autobahn at very low levels; it looked to me like they were at about one hundred meters. I guessed that they were practicing landings on the autobahn without actually landing. I didn't normally cover air targets, but this was just too blatant. I had Smitty pull into the median and stop. I got on top of the G-wagon and started photographing the Foxbats as they flew over.

I did this for about fifteen minutes when I looked down the autobahn at the oncoming traffic and saw another G-wagon approaching. I guess they saw me about the same time because they swerved into the median and began slowing down. I realized they were coming much too fast and were not going to get stopped. I began looking for someplace to jump, but at the very last moment they swerved around us. When they finally got stopped they backed up (Milton and SFC Terens), and we had a good laugh about the close call.

I am not much of a collector of Soviet memorabilia, but, as I got closer to the end of my third year and thought I might be transferred from the Mission, I decided I wanted a Soviet officer's hat—a new one. We happened to have a small social function with the officers from SERB held at the USMLM Potsdam House. I was talking with Major Stefan Maltsev and mentioned that I would like to trade for such a hat. He said he thought that he could make that work, so I asked what he wanted. He said he would like a US BDU hat and a bag of Bic pens for his two daughters to take to school. We agreed on the exchange and agreed to meet the following week at the Potsdam house.

I got the hat, but as luck would have it, the PX was out of Bic pens that week. So I bought some Parker pens instead. When we met the following week he had the hat that I wanted and he liked the BDU hat—but he didn't want the Parker pens. He said his daughters would just lose them, so he would wait for Bic pens. So, when the PX finally got Bic pens, I bought a bag and just carried them with me. I knew I would run into him again at some point.

A couple of weeks later, I was on the local with Smitty, and we were driving on Route 2, which ran through the garrison of the 34th Guards Artillery Division. There was a bus stop at the garrison front gate, and, as we drove by, I noticed MAJ Maltsev standing at the bus stop. I had Smitty do a U-turn and return to the bus stop. He did another U-turn in front of the bus stop to put me on the side with MAJ Maltsev. Now, picture this: We are in an obviously military vehicle with US Markings. We are both wearing US military uniforms with US Flags on the shoulders. We do two conspicuous U-turns and I jump out of the vehicle, shake MAJ Maltsev's hand and hand him a brown paper bag. Then Smitty and I drive away. I know Maltsev spent the next fifteen minutes explaining what that was all about to the other Soviet officers at the bus stop. Smitty and I laughed about it the rest of the way up the street.

Speaking of Smitty, he was an interesting character. He was a young black guy who had been born in Berlin to a military family and spoke near perfect German. He went to high school in Berlin and had married a German girl and had a beautiful little girl. I toured a lot with Smitty. One time we were transiting Wittenburg and somehow managed to get two flat tires. Smitty found a phone somewhere and called for help. It was a warm, sunny day, and we knew it would take a couple of hours for someone to bring us new tires. We made ourselves comfortable and settled in to wait. It was late afternoon, and young people from the town began walking by. Smitty engaged some of them and asked where they were all going. They told him there was a disco around the corner and they were all going dancing. Smitty was a young guy, and the girls were all fascinated by him. Most had never seen a black guy before. Finally one of the girls asked if she could rub his head. He started laughing and told me what was going on and asked if it would be okay. I said, "Sure." So, for the next half hour, about twenty or thirty young girls came out of the disco to rub Smitty's head.

I mentioned earlier that Clyde Evans was one of the class pranksters when we were going to the Naval Postgraduate School and to the US Army Russian Institute. One afternoon I was headed out on the local with Smitty as my driver. As we pulled up to the Soviet checkpoint on Glienicke Bridge and we handed our documents to the Soviet guard, I heard Smitty say to the guard, "Ya yem govno."

I knew Smitty did not speak Russian and had no clue what he was saying, but he got a big grin from the guard; so I let it go for the moment. After we cleared the bridge, I asked Smitty where he had learned the phrase. He told me that he had been working with Clyde to learn a couple of Russian phrases that he could use with the bridge guards. This was the first of the phrases that Clyde had taught him, and he was getting big grins from the bridge guards every time he used it. No wonder, "Ya yem govno" means "I eat sh*t."

I laughed and did not tell him what it meant for another couple of weeks.

Chapter 21
Senior Year

Through a set of circumstances, not necessarily attributable to myself, I wound up being the most experienced tour officer at the mission in my third year. Of my contemporaries at the Mission, Clyde had gone off to be a battalion commander of a tank battalion in West Germany, John Eschrich had been assigned as Ground Operations Officer, Paul Nelson had assumed the position of Mission Executive Officer, and Nick Nicholson was the Ground Production Officer; all of the other tour officers had come from later USARI classes. The air team likewise had replaced virtually everyone during my junior year and the same was true of the NavRep. So I wound up being the most experienced tour officer simply by lasting longer than anyone else. It didn't bother me at all—I loved being a tour officer. But there were a couple of perks and responsibilities that went along with that unofficial designation.

The main perk was that there was an intelligence conference held for a week in London every year (US/Brits), to which both the US and Brits sent a senior tour officer. Wives were invited, so it was a very nice trip. I didn't have to make any kind of presentation; I was just there as a reference source if they needed one, so it was easy to prepare for. And I love London. It was a great perk.

The responsibilities were focused on the new tour officers. I wound up backseating with just about everyone, which was enjoyable from the standpoint that I got to know everyone pretty well but also spent about as much time preparing for a tour as I did my own tours. The good side was that they had to write up their own tour reports, and the guidance on reports came mostly from the production officer. I only insisted on making sure that they updated the target folders. In addition to training the new ground tour officers, the air team was short on experienced tour personnel, so I backseated with them some also.

Not every training tour went perfectly. In an earlier chapter, I mentioned backseating with Major Skip Bohn at a SA-5 site near Rostock and relearned the rule about "never going back" and nearly got rammed by a dump truck.

I was with Todd Milton on one of his training tours, and I was not paying close attention to our navigation, when suddenly I saw the end of a runway go by that I had never seen before and realized that I had let him run us into a PRA. (Lesson learned: never trust anyone else's navigation.) That could happen almost anytime that you depended even on anyone else—even our most experienced NCOs. I was with Jesse Schatz, one night, who knew East Germany like the back of his hand. We had been going all day long and I was tired. Jesse was also, and we should have pulled off somewhere and taken a nap. I drifted off to sleep, only to wake up suddenly and see the city limits sign for Wittstock go by—which meant that we were well into the Wittstock PRA.

I reflected back on the advice given by Colonel Greenwalt, my first Chief of Mission during my rookie year, that a tour officer's perception of when he was in danger narrowed into smaller and smaller zones the longer he toured until finally some tour officers lost all fear—which was a dangerous situation because you needed enough fear to generate caution. And I realized that he was right. My perception of when we were in danger had narrowed considerably. I knew enough ways in and out of almost every target that I felt if we were just alert we could escape any situation. I even felt that my detentions gave me confidence that if I did get caught that I could defuse the situation safely. I had developed what I could only call a sixth sense of when something bad was about to happen. I did not realize how much I relied on this sixth sense until the following year when I became the ground operations officer and only toured about one-third as often as I did my first three years. I discovered that with the lower level of touring I had lost much of that sixth sense.

I never stopped doing some things that I learned in my rookie year. I never stopped looking for new and different routes in and out of targets, and I think I learned something new on every tour. I never stopped working on my vehicle recognition skills. I never stopped practicing blowing off surveillance. In fact, I came to view blowing off surveillance as an art form. Even when it was a quiet tour, you could almost always count on two or three surveillance vehicles. When you were bored it could add a touch of excitement to an otherwise eventless day. I remember being with Randy Everett, and we had identified several surveillance vehicles, including a nice new BMW that the Stassies had probably confiscated from some West German; and which we could definitely not out run on the autobahn. There was only one thing we could do. We found a spot with a steep downhill grade off of the autobahn and just turned and went straight down. I was sure they would not try to manage the steep grade in their sedans—especially the BMW—and I was right. We drove down the slope and across a plowed field. We looked back at the autobahn and there were three vehicles, including the BMW, stopped with half a dozen guys standing on the side of the road with their hands on their hips watching us disappear onto the side roads.

One of the downsides of my senior year was that I knew very quickly into a tour whether it would be exciting or boring. Boring tours had a potential to get us into trouble because I began looking for things to make the tour of value, and that usually involved getting close to a garrison.

For example, one very hot evening just after sunset, Dave Boone and I were sitting in a forested area near the Jueterbog PRA and training area. As we ate, the Sovs began firing artillery illumination rounds inside the training area. I noticed that about every fifth or sixth illumination round did not go off at the same altitude as the others. So I began counting them and recording the failure rate. It was very low key. They fired for a couple of hours, and I counted for a couple of hours. When we returned from the tour, it was the only IIR (Intelligence Report) I was asked to write from that tour. Not exciting but it had some value.

Another situation, again with Dave Boone, it was late night—after midnight—and there was a rail offload going on at the Gross-Ammensleben rail siding. It was a tank regiment—not particularly sexy, just a regiment of T-64s going home. We were watching from a wood line, first about five hundred meters away. Then we moved closer to about two hundred meters. Finally, as the last tanks pulled out of the rail siding, we drove passed the siding and then followed them down the tac trail for a distance. The tac trail led into the PRA, so we couldn't go far, and really, we had gotten everything, including photos from five hundred meters.

Dave was Special Forces, which I liked and didn't like. The SF guys were fearless. They didn't get overstressed in a chase. But they didn't get stressed when they should. I knew that I could depend on Randy Everett or Steve Eair-heart or Ron Blake to react to a Sov guard or vehicle immediately. I left security and the decision to break contact in their hands. If I knew things were going to go bad and I wanted them to wait until the last minute, I would warn them and they would adjust. But their skittishness got us out of danger. The SF guys didn't think we were in trouble until we had guns pointed at us. Dave and I were slipping into the Koenigsbruek Training Area on a tac trail from the west side. As we entered the training area on the tac trail, a ZIL-131 drove right passed us going the opposite direction. Dave just looked at me, at which point I told him to get us out of here as I watched the ZIL in the rear view mirror trying to get turned around. Dave just grinned at me. Everett or Eair-heart would have already been gone.

One of the things that was fun to do was drive by the Airborne Battalion at Cottbus (just south of Luebben and a ways north of Dresden). There wasn't much to it. If you were transiting south from Berlin to the Dresden area, it was on your way and easy to do. The garrison was right on the main road, set back about five hundred meters from the road. Now, Airborne units are pretty basic, without much equipment other than small arms, mortars, and rocket launchers. On a drive by you might see several light reconnaissance vehicles and maybe a GAZ-66 light truck towing a 120mm Mortar setting out front of the garrison. But the fun thing was that they had a small training area about two kilometers southwest of the garrison where they practiced jumps. The training area was about a kilometer square on the opposite side of the highway from the garrison, so you couldn't miss them if they were doing practice jumps. A couple of times during a drive-by I could see three or four helicopters hovering over the training area with troops jumping from the doors. It was a simple exercise, not tactical at all. About ten or twelve jumpers would jump, the helicopter would land, pick up another load, hover straight up to the jump height, let the jumpers jump, and do it all over again. It was so low key that, although they must have seen us from the air, they did not bother to send any one to chase us off. After watching for about an hour it was time to move on.

Being a political science major in college, it has always been interesting to me that, despite their avowed philosophical foundations, virtually every socialist country treats their people worse than do capitalist countries. And it is not a small difference—it is big. I think the only national success that the

Soviets could claim is that they took a largely illiterate nation to near one hundred percent literacy in seventy years. And yes, they had a powerful military force that allowed them to threaten other nations or, more realistically, kept other nations from intruding on their sphere of influence. But building and maintaining that force was clearly at the expense of other parts of their economy. And this was not just in the Soviet Union. Although there were brighter spots in the rest of the Warsaw Pact, they all suffered from this situation.

The most obvious evidence of this was the dinginess that was everywhere. I read these types of comments as a student at Oklahoma State and later at the Naval Postgraduate School but saw it for myself as I began traveling to various destinations in Eastern Europe and the Soviet Union while attending USARI. The socialist countries were gray. Cross the border from a western country on a bus and it was immediately apparent. The brightness of Western cities and villages disappeared and the world turned gray. Buildings never looked clean and bright, they always looked like the day they were brand new, the paint had faded. Streets were dirty and filled with potholes especially away from the main streets. Even the people looked tired and gray, as if every day was a constant struggle that never let up. East Germany was no different, but there were a couple of places that really struck me as terrible.

Halle. South of Dresden and home of the 27th GMRD, it also had a chemical plant (I think their main product was paint) that spewed a fine gray ash that simply covered the city. The whole city—buildings, parks, trees, cars, buses—was covered with a layer of gray two shades dirtier than any place I had ever been. This was not just around the factory but over the whole city. It was there when we drove passed the city limits sign and was everywhere until we left. Every time that I went there I felt like I was inhaling poison the whole time. I could not imagine what the citizens of the city felt like or what the normal life span of a citizen of Halle was.

North of Dresden and south of Cottbus near the Polish border was an area that we never seemed to visit or target, and I always wondered what was there. So, one early morning when things were slow and I was touring with Jesse Schatz and we were in the general area, I asked Jesse if he knew what was there. He said he had no idea either, so I decided to kill a couple of hours looking around. There was a small village on the map and I figured we could find a bakery and get some fresh rolls for breakfast anyhow.

We headed east down a two-lane paved road, but it was extremely foggy with visibility so restricted that I got out of the G-wagon and walked in front of it to guide Jesse. I am glad that I did.

Just about where I thought we should have encountered the first buildings of the town there was a dead drop-off of well over two hundred feet. No warning signs, no barriers, just a sudden drop off where the edge of the town should have been according to our map. It was a large quarry. Just thinking about what could have happened if we had not been proceeding at walking speed scared me to death.

Another example of environmental disregard that always startled me is what happened during tactical training. In the West, tactical exercises are tightly controlled. If in the course of a tactical exercise a tank or other vehicle accidentally (or purposefully) damages, even slightly, a farmer's field or a forested area, the farmer or forest meister has established recourse to make a claim for losses from the damage. In East Germany where the fields and forests are collectively owned nobody seemed to care. The Sovs pretty much stuck to their established tac trails but if needed they did not hesitate to turn into a farmer's field if necessary. I will say that after three years of touring it was clear to me that forest meisters did not like the fact that the Sovs used their forests for bivouac sites and bunker locations. It seemed clear to me that they very much enjoyed harvesting trees around bunkers and vehicle revetments, rendering them useless as emergency deployment sites.

One advantage to us was that, because most things were owned collectively, there were few fences around fields which made every plowed or un-plowed field a potential escape route. The only place we really had to be careful was the small personal plots near every village, where private individuals grew vegetables and fruits. They were almost always fenced, and we were all careful about those.

The East German people as a group hated the Sovs, and it was not unusual for them to point out the location of units deployed in the area if we were driving through. And it was not unusual for them to flag us down while we were driving by, just to tell us that they wanted the US to keep up the pressure on the Sovs, as long as they were in East Germany. On the other hand, if they thought that we were in the area to work against a local East German unit, they would report us in a minute. It was just another reason I didn't like doing East German targets.

As my senior year progressed, I began helping John Eschrich with the Ground Operations Officer's responsibilities. John was working pretty hard and did not have a backup and I was interested, so it kind of worked out. He took a couple of vacations, and I covered for him and decided I liked it. I knew infantry branch was just going to send me to an ROTC assignment if they got me, so I called the FAO assignments officer and asked if they would talk to the infantry guys about leaving me at the Mission for another year as the ground ops officer. John was being groomed to be the Chief of Ground, and John and I worked well together, so I thought it would be a good assignment. The FAO guys were sure that they could work it out, so I settled in for another year in Berlin. I figured that as ground ops officer I would be able to control my own touring schedule and keep myself on the road. I was wrong about that.

Chapter 22
Year 4 - Ground Operations Officer

Just as I transitioned into ground operations, personal computers became the rage and I became fascinated with them. The Mission was provided with a TEMPEST-secured Apple computer, which we had no idea what to do with. Whatever the official purpose was, I noticed that it had a database program loaded on it, and it seemed to me that loading our target list into a database might help us manage it better. I assigned one of our NCOs (Ron Blake) the responsibility of loading basic information into the computer about each target in our target file. It couldn't replace the target folders, but it could help us keep track of how frequently we were covering targets and prioritizing them. Colonel Lajoie worried that the computer would be used to actually generate target lists for tour teams and could actually put teams at risk by targeting them against targets that had been overly sensitized, and while I suppose we could have used it to actually generate target lists, neither Ron nor I were sophisticated enough database users to do that. We just used it to keep track of the number of times a target had been covered and the last date of coverage. We also set it up to allow us to highlight particularly sensitive targets. When preparing a target list, we would run a prioritized list of all targets not covered since a certain date. Prioritization was more or less a function of what the ground production officer wanted covered. We would then review that list and pick a series of targets within reasonable proximity of each other that also gave us pretty wide coverage of an area as the team transited from the Potsdam

House through the assigned target list. This was a bit of an art form as, at least while I was the ground ops officer, my objective for tours was to generally cover major installations and training areas once each time we were in an area and during the course of about a week ensure that a USMLM team drifted through each part of the area watching for general activities.

So, from this list of general targets that the computer generated, we would pick a series of targets for a team that gave us good coverage of an area. Of course, the objective was to find and observe any ongoing activity, so the status of the Sov training schedule played a role in our planning as well. Targets were picked to place teams in expected areas of activity.

As a tour officer I averaged fifty tours a year, and I was hopeful to maintain that pace while I was the ops officer but it just wasn't possible. There was simply too much to do. So my fourth year I did about fifteen tours. I learned two things as ops officer that I paid serious attention to when it came to touring. First, I noticed how tired people were sometimes. The touring schedule was rigorous, and stresses on the road were real. Adrenalin highs got you through lots of tight spots but contributed in the long run to general tiredness. If you asked a tour officer or NCO if he was tired, the answer was always "no," but they were. Second, I discovered that the sixth sense that I had finely honed as a tour officer, which told me that trouble was coming even though I couldn't see it, was dependent on regular use. At fifteen tours per year, it was not there. I was much more cautious when touring as the ops officer than as a tour officer. I learned that given this loss of sensitivity, it was better to leave sensitive targets to full-time tour officers. I would have liked to have listened to my pride and toured as aggressively as I did my first three years but that would have stupidly placed myself and driver at unnecessary risk.

As fate would have it, the tour that Nick was shot on was the first tour that I sent out in my new capacity as ground operations officer. I have gone through the planning for that trip and there was nothing unusual about it. I walked it through with his driver, Jesse Schatz, and they did not do anything different or unusual about their actions in running the target list. Ludwigslust was not even a primary target. It was a backup target once they confirmed that there was nothing left to cover at the North Elbe River Crossing site. It was a normal enough tour, except for the outcome. But once it happened, it affected our operations for the whole year that followed.

I was angry at the Sovs for having shot Nick. If it had been up to me, every tour officer with credentials would have been on the road the next morning. I was going to prove that no brazen act of stupidity on their part could keep us from doing our job. Rightly or wrongly, others prevailed and we pulled everyone off the road for a week while the press uproar continued and preparations for Nick's funeral were made. It was such an emotional whirlwind that, although I was there as a pall-bearer, I have no memory of the funeral. I remember the flight to Andrews Airbase on a military aircraft and spending a few minutes alone with Nick's casket in the back of the aircraft but that is it. I don't remember anything else. I do remember getting on a commercial airliner at Dulles International Airport and going to sleep as we taxied to the runway, and I did not wake up until the plane hit the runway at Frankfurt.

I was not involved in the negotiations surrounding Nick's death in any way. My job along with John Eschrich (now Chief of Ground) was to get the ground team back in action. We coordinated every step with the British and French Missions. I met weekly with Major Simon Cleveland and Major Dan Trastour so that we were well aware of what each team was doing and monitoring Sov responses.

On the surface, we were basically in a "walk on eggshells" mode. The negotiations were often vitriolic, and no one wanted it to get worse because of another incident.

I would guess that it is a tribute to the value of the contributions made by USMLM and SMLM that no one suggested just closing the Missions down. At least that is the way that I took it, and I used this as my guideline. What we were doing before was highly valued in our Intelligence Community, so much so that, even then, no one was pushing to close the Mission. So we returned to our basic targeting with the caveat that we directed tour teams not to press too hard. It was not difficult to enforce. Tour teams were *always* careful.

The one thing that became clear, regardless of what the Soviets said, was that, until the very end of the negotiations, the instructions to their soldiers concerning how they were to react to Mission teams did not change. Responses to teams remained about the same. There was even another shooting in which a member of the USMLM air team was slightly wounded later in the summer.

An interesting aspect of this whole affair was that for about two weeks our Mission and details of our activities were widely discussed in the press. I am sure this happened to everyone at the Mission, but I was peppered with questions from my family and friends about activities described in the paper and Time Magazine. At the same time, we had all been reminded that our mission and activities were still classified, so we were not at liberty to discuss the very things described in the press. It made for some interesting conversations.

It was an interesting aside to my assignment as the Ground Ops Officer at USMLM that, at virtually the same time, the USAREUR liaison office to the Soviet Military Liaison Mission operating in West Germany was headed by Major Dirk Wyckoff. Dirk was also a Soviet FAO a year behind me at the US Army Russian Institute and, while not directly related, he is a good friend. But both his organization and USMLM reported to the same office in USAREUR. He was physically located there and came to their mind anytime someone identified themselves as Major Wyckoff on the phone. On several occasions I called to report or respond to a request from USAREUR, only to get halfway through the conversation and realize that they thought they were talking to Dirk. I would have to stop, remind them that I was Tom Wyckoff, and we would start over.

About half way through my year as ground ops officer, Colonel Lajoie moved to a new assignment; and a new Chief of Mission, Colonel Bill Haloran, arrived from his last assignment as the Army Attaché in Moscow. He and his wife were two of the most genuinely nice people I have ever met. But he had apparently been tasked by someone in the chain of command to bring some structure to the Mission. At any rate, we began writing a standard operating procedure (SOP) to provide direction to tour teams for various situations. As I have mentioned before, if I had a criticism of the mission, it was that our training process left a lot to the imagination, and initially I thought this SOP could fill some of that gap. But it soon became a nightmare. Every situation that occurred was investigated and a "proper" course of action determined and an SOP written. It was quite an education in human relations for me. As it became clear that every close call was going to result in the generation of a new paragraph in the SOP, incident reporting began to dry up. It wasn't that anyone cared about a new SOP, it was that the tour teams were expected to remember and follow the steps identified in the SOP. The situations that teams got into were so varied that no SOP could cover them all. But rather that simply try to provide general guidelines for touring, the SOP tried to provide specific instructions: when to break off coverage, how close to get, when to stop, etc. As OPS officer I noticed there were fewer discussions between tour teams. They were sharing less. I began to sense that rules/guidelines were being ignored. On tour I tried to get the NCOs to chat with me about the SOP guidelines and how they were being applied—whether or not they were helpful—but the NCOs weren't saying much. So my perception was that the guidelines were being selectively ignored. That made me nervous because my experience told me that when people began to decide for themselves which rules they would follow and which they would ignore the gray areas varied from person to person and sometimes were quite large.

The Mission was not well suited to specific rules and guidelines because every situation was different to one degree or another. It was better suited to general guidelines for the ground team like:

- Before you start in on a target, determine if you are under surveillance and, if so, blow them off.
- If you can't blow your surveillance, abort the target.
- Do your best to cover your target without being seen.
- Once you are seen, be prepared to leave quickly.
- If you are seen by a guard with a weapon, and he reacts to your presence, it is time to go
- If your driver observes a threatening change in your security situation, make sure he knows to break off coverage immediately.
- In the event that you are being pursued, secure all equipment.
- If it appears that further efforts to escape could result in damage to the vehicle or injury to yourselves or those pursuing you, it is time to accept the detention.
- Never assume that you are one hundred percent safe or secure.
- Do not violate PRAs or TRAs without prior authorization.
- Remember that if you are behind MRS signs Sovs consider you to be "fair game."
- Remember that if you are out of the vehicle you are ten times more vulnerable.
- Know your target (prepare) in order to properly assess the risks you are taking in any situation versus the potential gain.
- Remember there are 100,000 of them and fourteen of us—and they have guns!

- Beyond general guidelines like these, the reason that we handpicked captains and majors from USARI was that they came with experience and good judgment built-in. They had families and were not going to take unnecessary risks.

Fortunately for me, about the time that the SOP was becoming a significant concern, I was reassigned.

I had called the FAO assignments officer and asked if they could get me a position in the Washington, D.C. area. My wife and I had been in Germany for six years, and we were ready to get back to the land of round doorknobs and electric garage door openers. I was sure my infantry career was dead, so I asked the FAO guys to get me something that would give me some greater experience as a FAO. It worked out great from my perspective. As I have mentioned earlier, I was assigned as Chief of the Warsaw Pact Order of Battle Section in the Defense Intelligence Agency (DIA)—a major consumer of USMLM reporting. I had thirty-five analysts that kept track of every tank, truck, and kitchen trailer that was held by the Warsaw Pact forces. Information provided by the Mission provided the order of battle template for units throughout the Warsaw Pact. It is another story entirely, but in this position I learned how important the collection efforts of USMLM really were.

In the long run, this had special meaning for me for two reasons. First, I worked routinely with analysts in the CIA and made a number of friends there. Second, the negotiations for the Conventional Forces in Europe (CFE) Treaty had taken a serious turn and my section became the most credible source of data about the Warsaw Pact for US Negotiators. That was particularly interesting because, after DIA, I was assigned as an action officer on the Joint Staff in J5 and spent half of my time in Brussels or Vienna as a part of the US Delegation to the CFE Negotiations.

As I continued my career in the military, my life at the Mission continued to follow me around. At DIA I learned that, having come from the mission, I could make a casual comment about a topic that an analyst had spent a couple of years researching using multiple intelligence sources and unintentionally and unknowingly undercut his research because of the high regard Mission personnel were held. I learned to keep quiet unless I was sure.

I was also selected to be one of the US Inspection team chiefs conducting inspections under the provisions of the Intermediate Nuclear Forces (INF)

Treaty and led or participated in twenty-six inspections of Soviet installations during the treaty baseline inspection period in the summer of 1988. Most of the team leaders were ex-tour officers from USMLM, and Paul Nelson and I were on the second flight into Moscow. (BG Lajoie and Larry Kelley were on the first inspection flight.) This baseline inspection period is probably worth another book all by itself, but, related to this book, I was told twice by Soviet military officers at the conclusion of the inspection that they had read my file and wanted to know if it was true that I had "done all those things in East Germany." Well, obviously I had not read that file and had no idea what it said, so I simply responded that I always did my best on any assignment I was given.

During the baseline I was targeted to inspect a location in East Germany at which SCUD missiles were deployed. First of all, the senior escort team leader for our inspection was Major Sergei Savchenko, whom I knew from my time at the Mission. He had been the senior Soviet interpreter during the negotiations following Nick's death, and we had become friends and spent a good amount of the transit period during the inspection talking about changes going on in the Soviet Union under Gorbachev and his policy of Glasnost. The site for our inspection was the installation of the 11th Guards Tank Division at Koenigsbruek, where I had many close calls and was detained once. I told Sergei I felt very uncomfortable entering the installation by the main gate. He got a laugh out of that. Sergei had also written a Russian version of the events surrounding Nick's death, which I have used as a reference.

As a known intelligence collector from my time at the Mission, security personnel clustered around me during the inspections, which, personally, I found challenging and interesting. But those are stories for another time.

Chapter 23

Conclusion

As I said at the beginning, this has simply been an effort to capture my personal memories of the time that I spent at the US Military Liaison Mission to the Group of Soviet Forces, Germany. It is a view of the Cold War from the perspective of a ground soldier who went out often on reconnaissance missions, unarmed, working with a number of other officers and NCOs from three countries against the largest, most well-equipped force that the major threat to the Western world could field. It was the best job that I ever had. It was personally challenging and rewarding. It was exciting. It suited me and qualified me well for a number of follow-on jobs that I also found rewarding.

Those who served as liaison offices in the three allied missions form a brotherhood that cannot be explained to others except in a general way. This book tells what we did and why, from my perspective. Others may agree or disagree. The reasons that we did what we did is tied up in the history of the Cold War. In that grand context of sixty years of hot and cold events, the Mission and its activities are now not much more than a footnote. I am confident that, had the Cold War ever gone hot, the liaison officers and NCOs of the allied missions would have been its first casualties. We would have seen the first initiatives on the part of Soviet forces. We would not have been allowed to return to report.

Operating in that environment, we provided good, reliable technical and order-of-battle reporting that was used by major intelligence agencies as a highly reliable source of information that could be used with other sources to build a good picture of the threat that faced the United States and NATO.

It was dangerous at times. The Mission and Cold War Berlin were exciting places to be in the 1980s—some serious and some not so serious situations occurred. I don't know if I have properly conveyed that sense of excitement and professional satisfaction that came with the job. I think I probably have conveyed a sense of things that happened to those who served that will jog their memories.

I do not want to suggest that the danger that we faced was anywhere near what American soldiers fighting in Iraq or Afghanistan face every day. We were unarmed, without communications, but facing a more predictable, civilized enemy.

I have not intended to criticize anyone in this book. There is not a name mentioned of a person that I do not respect and love. Each of those has as many stories as I have captured here, and some will have their own views of some events that are mentioned here that may differ from my memories. I am not apologetic. I set out to capture what memories I have, and I believe that they are as accurate as I can make them.

In the end, I ask myself was it all worth it? Particularly, my friend Nick's death? And I will say, "Yes." I believe that Nick's death was one of those events which ultimately led to the dissolution of the Soviet Union only a few years later. But in a general sense the contributions of mission personnel to the overall intelligence collection effort against the Soviet Union far outweighed the risks taken.

I will confess to becoming addicted to the adrenalin highs. I could not wait to get back on the road after every tour—not only because I wanted to collect intelligence but because I craved the excitement of the chases and close calls. If it was clear that a tour was going to be low key, I spent time seeking new routes around installations which I thought was a good use of my time but also gave the possibility of some excitement if personnel at the installation reacted. And blowing surveillance was always a thrill because they were almost always there. I think nearly every tour officer and NCO was similarly affected by this addiction.

I often asked myself if I was just imagining the dangers, but, as I reflect back on the French NCO Marriotti and Nick's deaths, the injuries or possible death of at least two Soviet soldiers, dozens of rammings and near rammings, ambushes, and wrecked vehicles, I would say that fear was often justified and a practical counter to the adrenalin highs. And I must believe that God had a hand in protecting me.

The one question I have most frequently asked myself about this time at the Mission is, "Why Nick?" Nick was very near the end of his tour at the Mission. There was nothing unusual about the site he was killed at—it was a secondary target on his target list. We had all been there before, many times. It was a Sunday afternoon and no training was in progress. Nick had a little girl and a wife that were left without a father and husband. The soldier fired the shots from an off-hand standing position and hit Nick with a deadly shot on his second shot. All factors that came together in one deadly moment. "Why Nick?" I don't suppose that anyone in this life will ever satisfactorily answer that question. It could have been any one of us.

There are many others that I have not mentioned in this short book that served at the Mission at the same time, and I am certain that if you locked us all in a room by ourselves for a day that more "war stories" would be told and remembered, and I could easily double the size of this book with them. I hope that for those who served at the Mission this brings back some memories or helps keep their memories fresh in their minds. As for me, I have told the stories that I most frequently remember when I think back on those years.

They were good years.